THE VideoBasics123 TRAINING SYSTEM

Handy Dandy WORKBOOK!

BASIC VIDEO TECHNIQUES

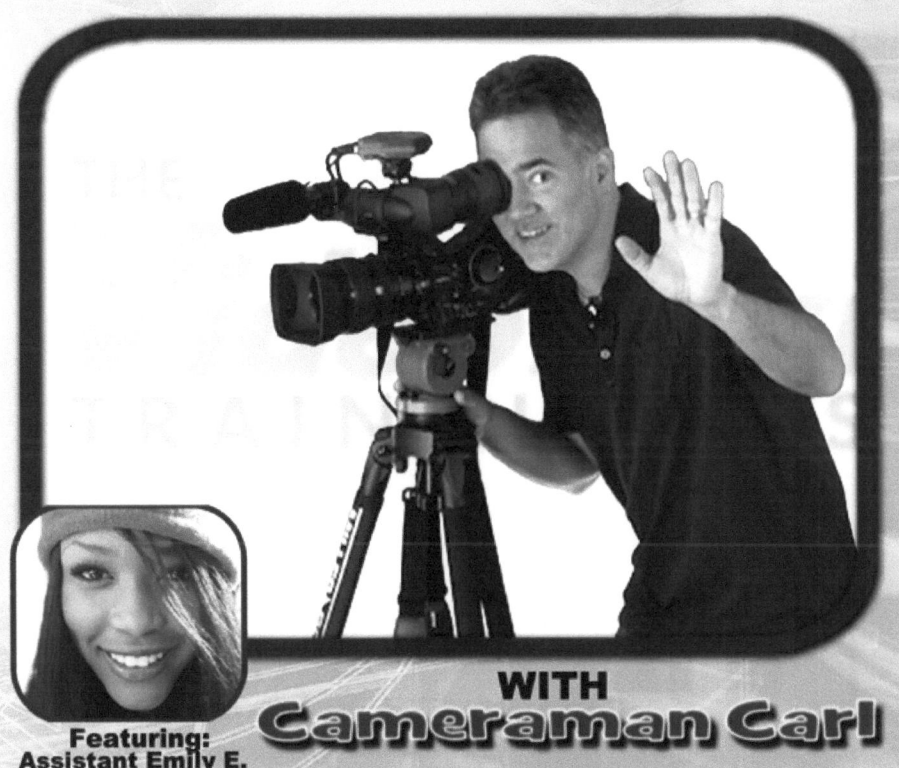

Featuring:
Assistant Emily E.

WITH Cameraman Carl

A Crown Broadcasting International Network, Inc. Publication – Copyright 2011

DEDICATION

The Crown Broadcasting family dedicates this workbook to all the multimedia enthusiasts out there who love and enjoy telling stories using video. We hope this training system is a great tool that will help you to shoot, edit and communicate those stories!

TABLE OF CONTENTS

ACKNOWLEDGMENTS

The Crown Broadcasting family would like to thank Dr. Phillip George Goudeaux for allowing our media team to shoot the "Big Give-Away Day" organized by Calvary Christian Center in Sacramento, California. Without his cooperation and encouragement we would not have been able to get the great shots that we did and be able to share this information with multimedia enthusiasts out there. Thanks again Dr. Goudeaux!

Also, a big thanks to the voice over talents of Emily E. She is a real trooper and spent countless hours of editing and just standing around and waiting. Emily E. you're a fantastic talent and great things are in store for you. We have to also give I big shout out to Tami Jones who put in many hours editing this workbook. Thanks ladies!

BASICS OF SHOOTING AUDIO

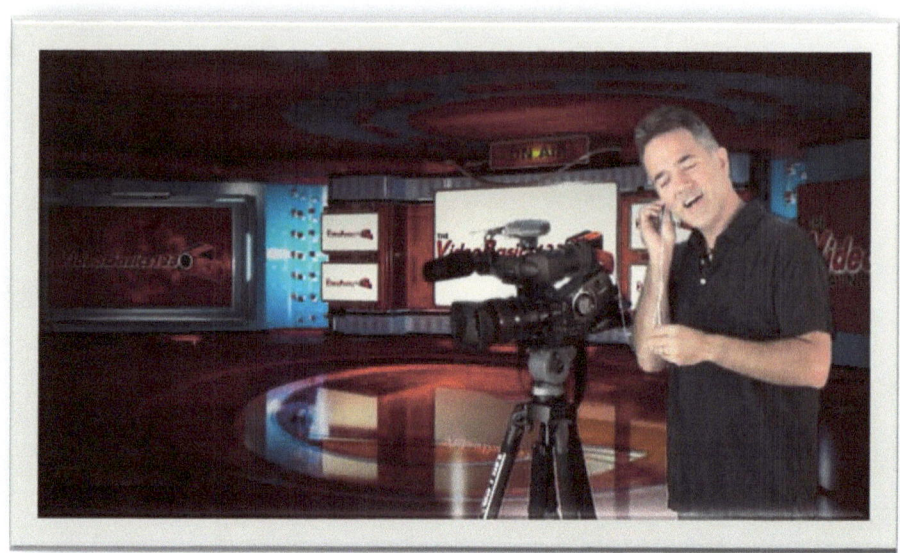

Audio is just as important as video. The picture has to be good and it has to make sense but if you can't hear what people are saying or hear the band playing then you're probably not going to pay much attention to the video.

If you can't hear me right now grab your remote and turn me up and listen to what I'm about to say. You must have good, clean, crisp, clear audio.

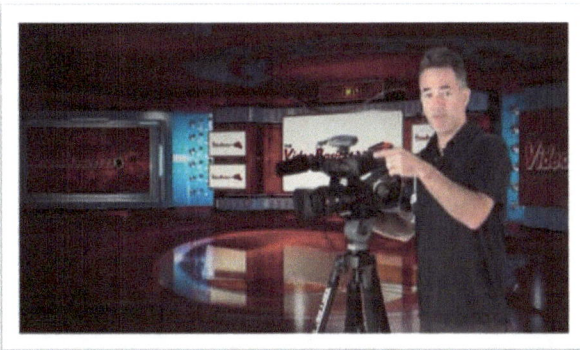

Now, you may not have one of these fancy microphones like the one I have on right now. You may not even have a boom mic like some lady at a major movie production.

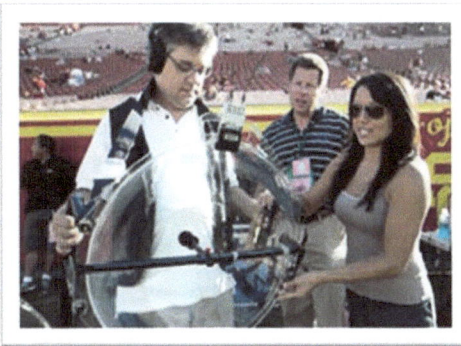

You may not be like the guy with a parabolic mic standing on the sidelines pointing at a crowd of athletes getting great sound, but I guarantee you I do know what you have. If you have a camera, then you have a shotgun microphone. A shotgun microphone sits somewhere on the front of your camera. Almost every single camera has a microphone, so I'm going to teach you how to use it.

3

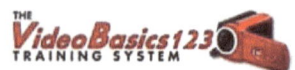

> ## CARL'S NOTES!
>
> Not all cameras are created equal. Some have small mics or big ones, but when it comes to capturing great audio, the principles are all the same. Let's head back to the studio so Carl can show you how to use your microphone the right way.

EVERY CAMCORDER IS UNIQUE!

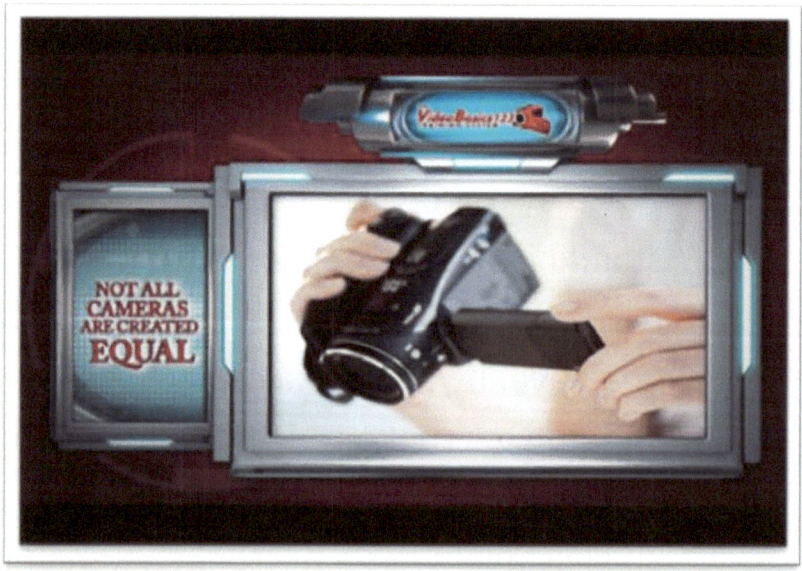

USING YOUR SHOTGUN MICROPHONE

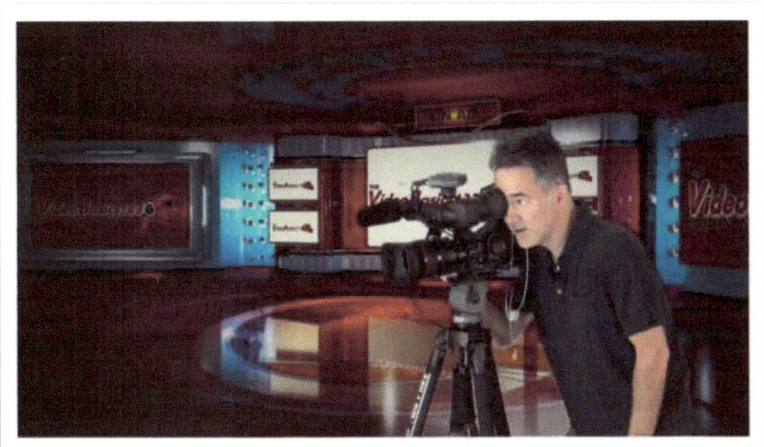

Now let's talk about the shotgun microphone. It's called a shotgun because it points out like a shotgun and it gathers sound going outward. It's similar to how a real shotgun fires. Sound can't be picked up forever, only a short distance but it goes farther than the lapel microphone I have on. It usually goes for a good ten feet for quiet people and beyond that, it's hard to tell.

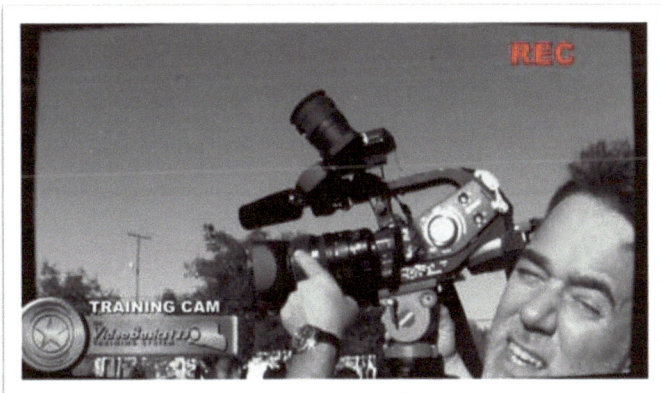

5

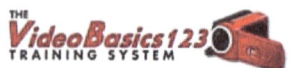

There is one great easy, simple way to tell if you can hear the sound with a shotgun microphone. Get a set of headphones and then you can hear what you're shooting.

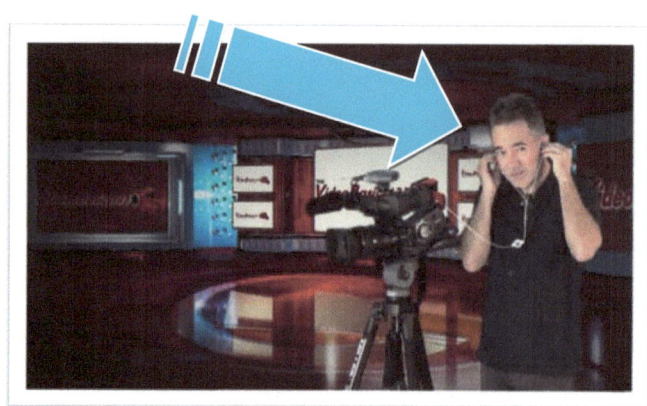

You don't have to put both head phones in because then you can't hear what's going on around you, but if you have at least one of them in most of the time, then you can tell if your shotgun mic is working right. And remember, if you're working the camera be very, very quiet. If you're next to your camera saying, "Oh, that was a great shot!" you're probably being picked up by your shotgun microphone. You're usually pretty close to the microphone and it can hear you!

Now, you're ready to go get some audio. Let's start with the interview. You want to talk to this guy. "Hey, how are you doing? Can I talk to you for a minute over here?"

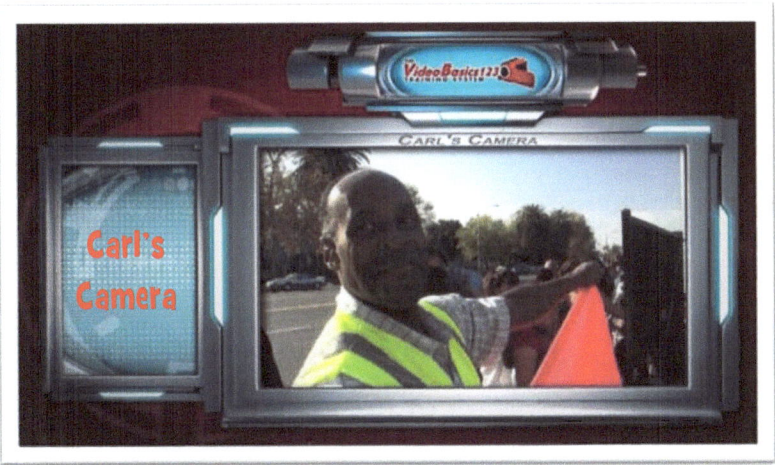

You attempt to set up this beautiful shot. Your subject is standing by some the trees that's only 20 feet away. There's cars over here driving by, kids playing nearby. It looks terrific. But you probably can't hear your subject because he's 20 feet away and there are other activities going on around you. You've got to get up nice and close. Remember, this is just for the shotgun microphone. It works best the closer you are.

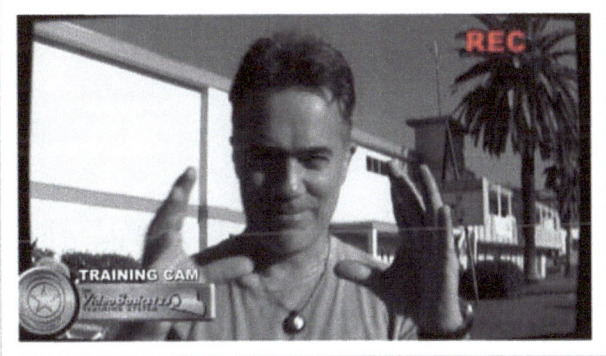

I suggest you zoom out all the way and then you walk up to the person. Not too close because you don't want to hit

7

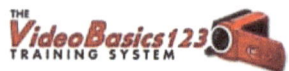

them in the nose. But walk up to the guy, speaking nicely to him so he's comfortable. Don't zoom into him. Keep your shot zoomed out as wide as possible.

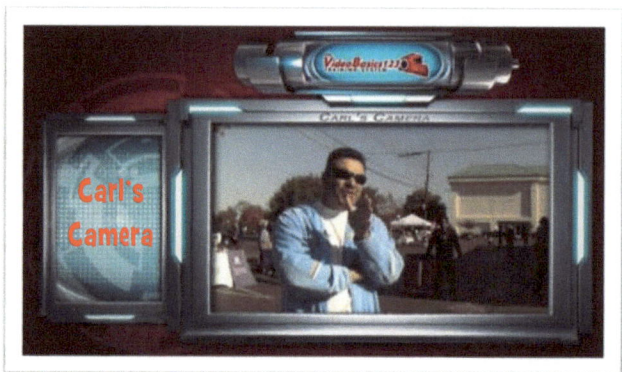

You want to walk up and frame your shot by walking up to your subject. I would suggest 2-3 feet away. It sounds close, but in your viewfinder it does not look that close. Your shotgun microphone should hear him with no problem. You'll know it's working because you have your headphones in.

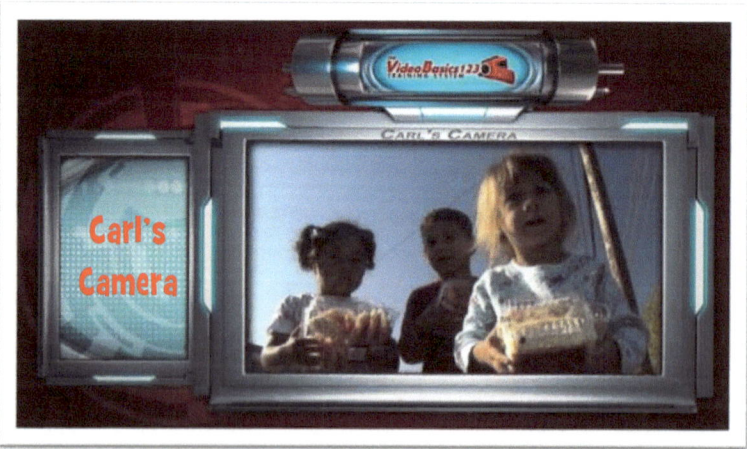

Once you get up nice and close and set your shot, don't worry too much about how awesome it is at that point because you can hear and see him. Now, just focus on asking him very simple questions. It's a great way to get an interview, especially if you only have a shotgun mic.

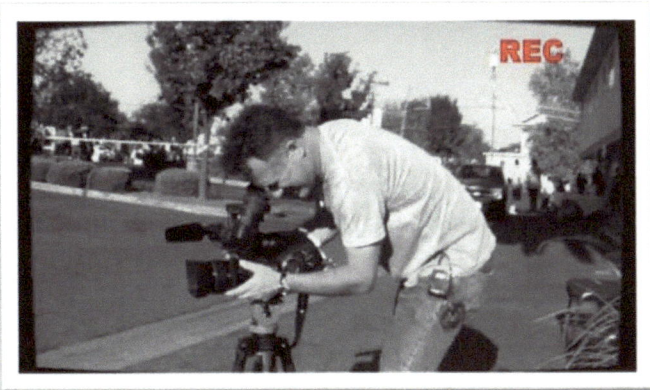

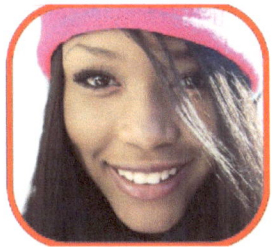

Carl's Assistant: **Now it's time for Carl to hit the streets with his "Training Cam". He visits a charity community event organized to help those in need. It's time to put his microphone to the test.**

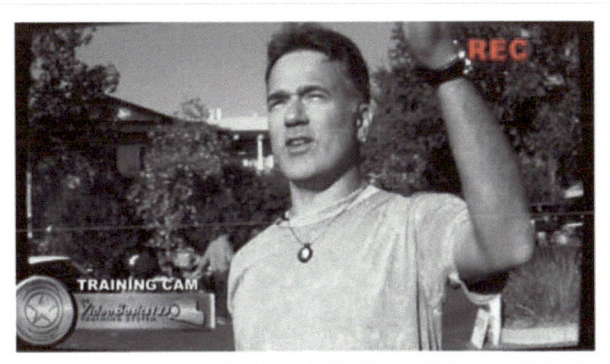

Carl: So we get here. The sun is right where I want it to be; right in my eyes. It's perfect that way. But as you may

9

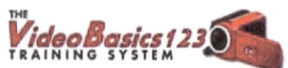

hear, there's music and it's loud because there's a deejay in the corner shouting. We'll have to watch out for that guy.

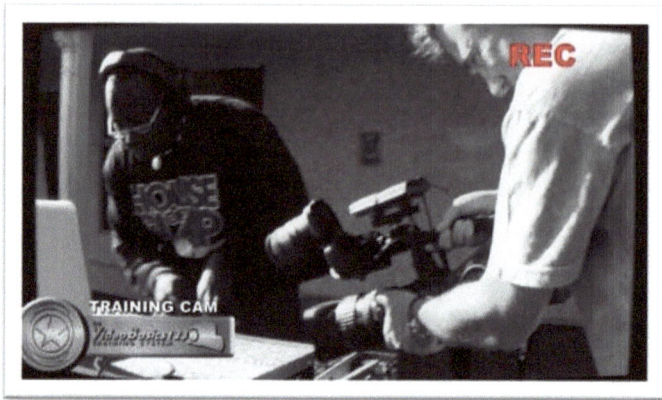

We're going use some of him later, but he might get a little too close to our interviews and our other natural sounds. So we're going to start backing away from the music and work our way back to the music just to get a little of both.

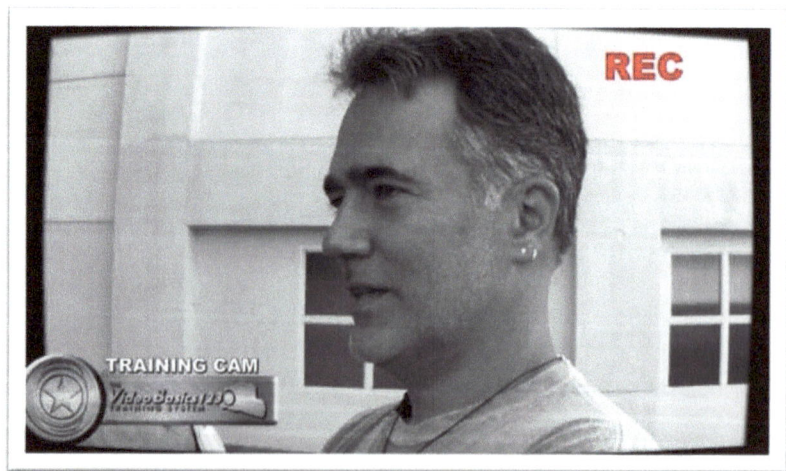

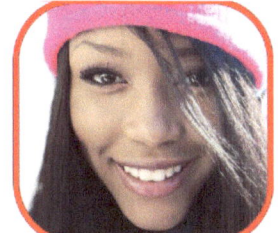

Carl's Assistant: There's a lot to consider when trying to get interviews in crowds or when there's a lot of traffic or if there's music nearby. That's why you have to get close to the people you're interviewing if you only have a shotgun microphone.

Notice how close Carl's camera is to the little boy. Remember, if you only have a shotgun microphone to pick up sound, you have to be close, especially when there's traffic or crowds around.

As Carl looks for more people to talk to, he's still carefully considering the music, crowds and other sounds in the area.

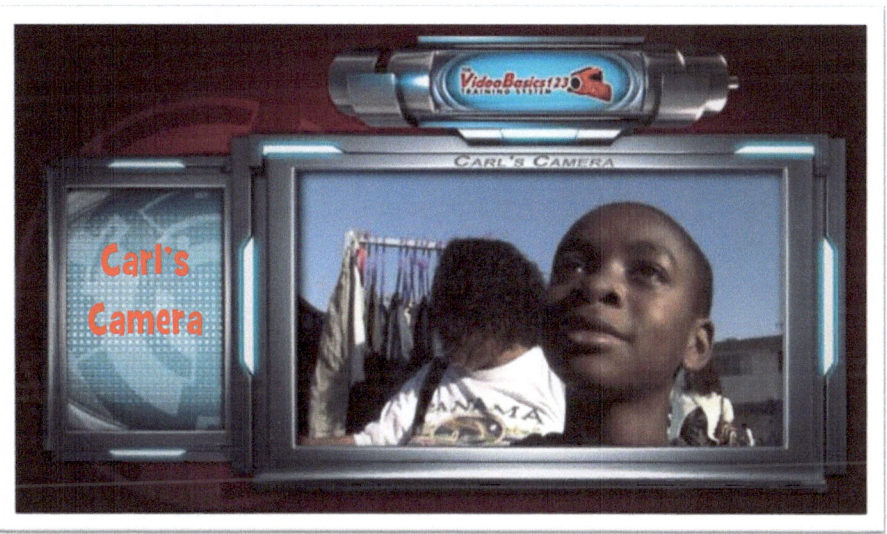

11

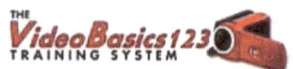

Okay. Here's a quick review. If you're talking to someone with the shotgun mic, remember to zoom out wide and get as close as possible and wear headphones to make sure you can hear properly then listen for other sounds around you.

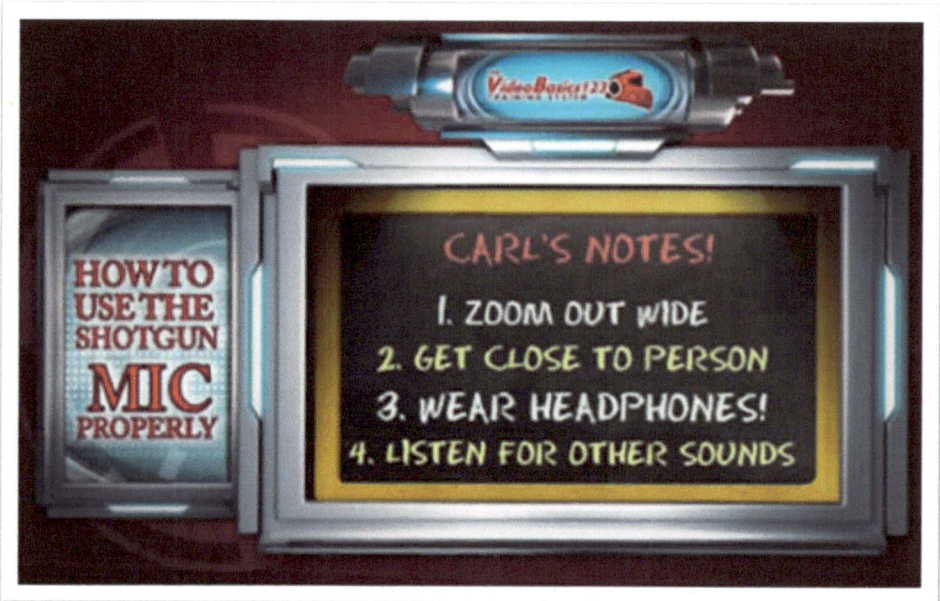

Capturing Natural Sound

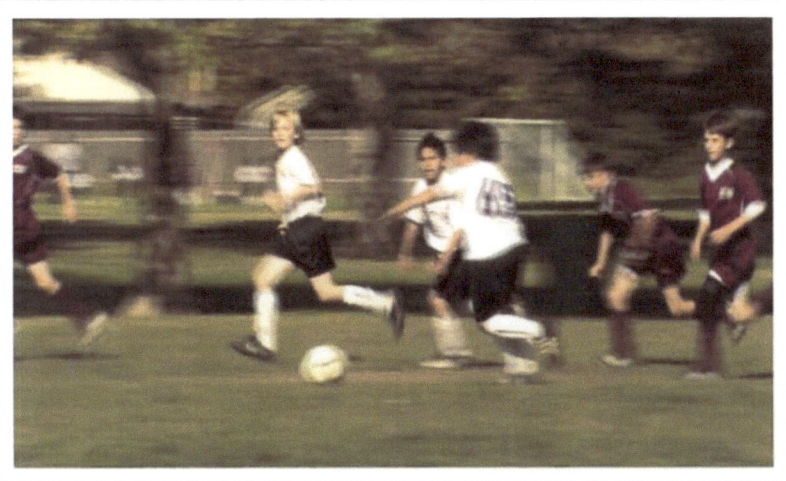

Let's move on to capture natural sounds. Natural sound can be anything from a sporting event to flying motorcycles or even a babbling brook. Natural sound puts the viewer in the moment and helps them get a clear picture. Capturing nature sound is an endless adventure!

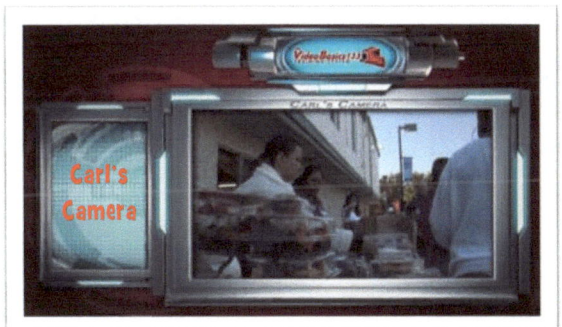

Let's say you're at your big event like a soccer game. Great! You're standing on the sidelines and you see all

13

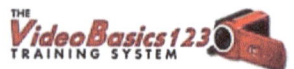

the kids playing and you want to get good sound at least one kid kicking the soccer ball. Well you can't just run out on the field because the ref might give you a penalty!

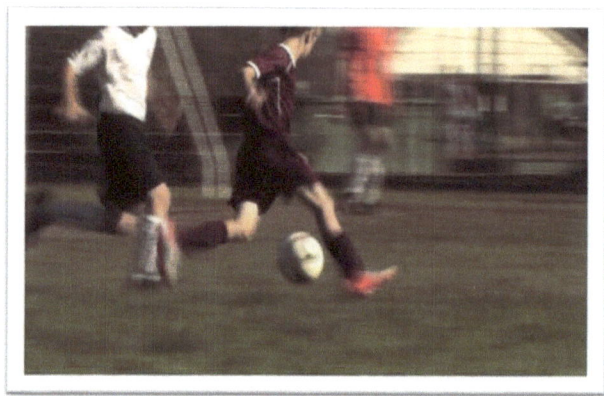

So, here's what you must do. Stay on the sidelines. As the players are coming close make sure your shotgun is as close to that field as you can get. Get those kids coming by kicking the ball.

If you're at the soccer game for your kid, pull your kid aside, get the camera down about a foot away and have him kick the ball. Guess what? You've captured the natural sound of their foot striking the ball. It's that easy!

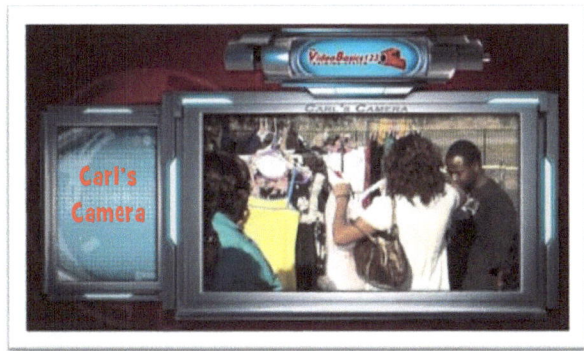

Later during editing you can add the sound of ball being kicked. Even though that shot is way across the field and you really can't hear it, you can cheat the sound in later.

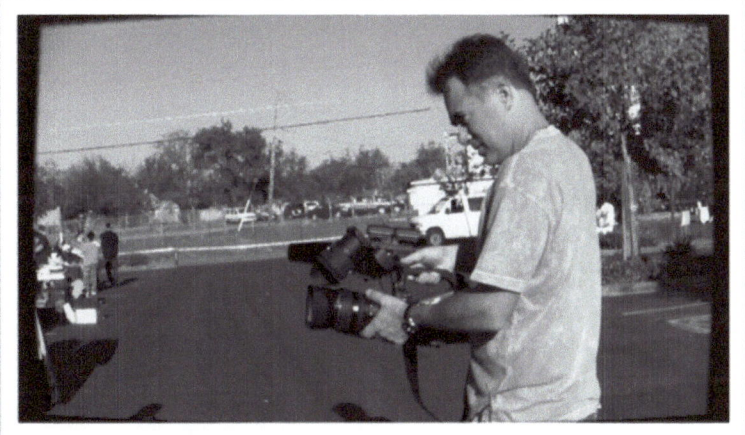

When capturing natural sounds you have to get close, just like in the interview. Get up nice and close. But, keep in mind you have to be careful, especially if you have lots of loud music or other noises in the area.

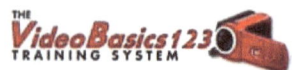

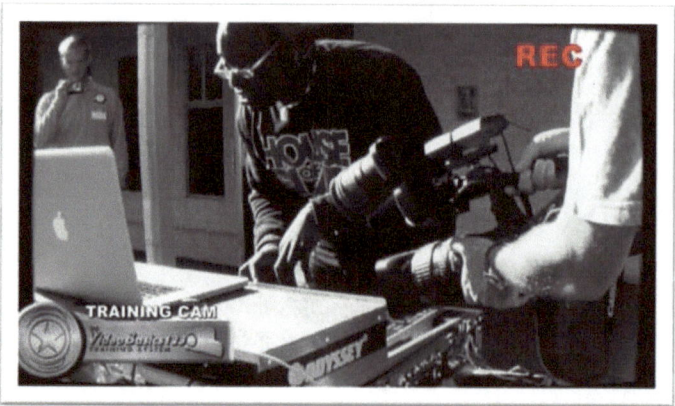

I notice you're getting close to the music now. It's not too loud, but I'm going to try and get some natural sounds. I need to get close otherwise the music is going to be too loud. Watch.

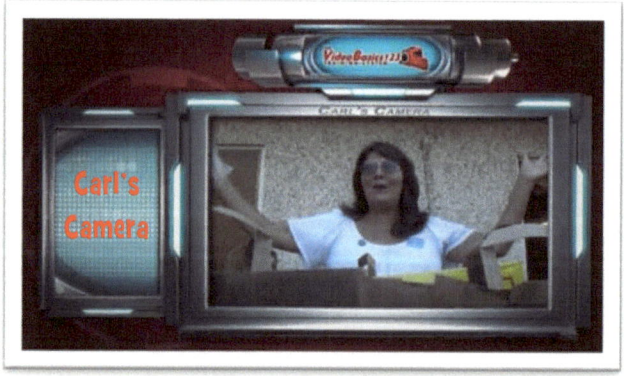

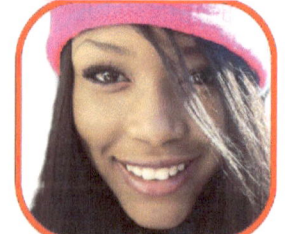 **Carl's Assistant: Carl is pretty close to the woman above. So, it's pretty easy to isolate her from other noises around her, but let's see what happens when Carl steps away from the lady and allows more sounds into the picture. You can hear the difference?**

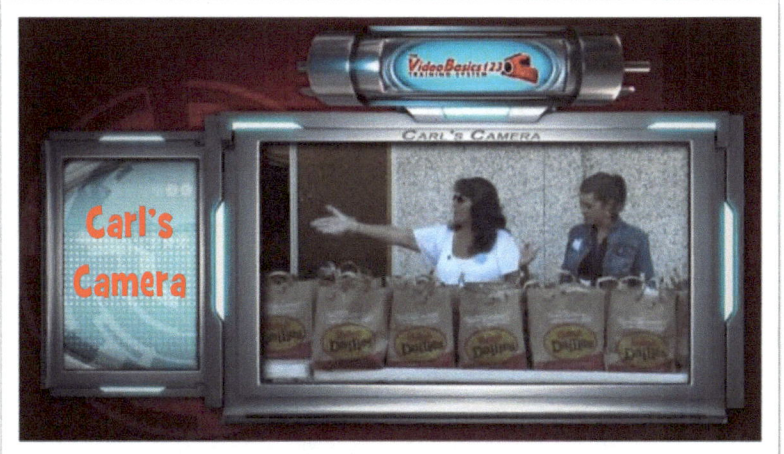

Carl: From here I can zoom in and I can see her just fine. But let's see what happens if I wanted to use the natural sound of her yelling, "cupcakes".

There's no way that's going to sound nearly as good as when I was closer. I'm Just too far away. She is screaming so it might show up a little, but not nearly as good as when I was right there.

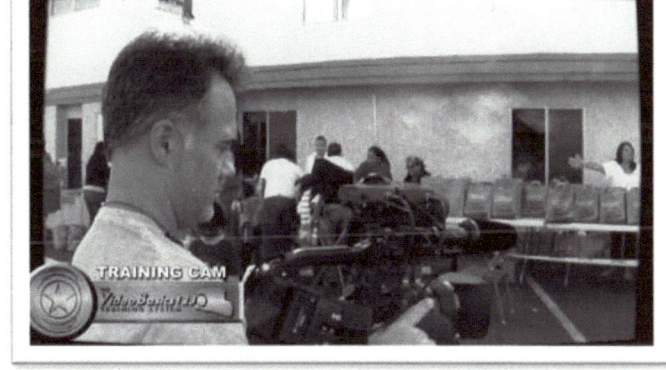

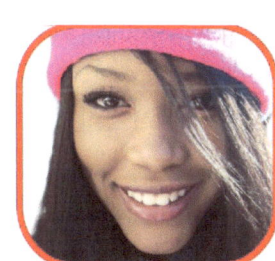

Carl's Assistant: Remember, while capturing natural sound with a shotgun mic you have to get close.

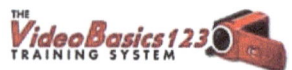

Carl: When there's music at an event, you can't ignore it. You've got to feel the beat and you have to shoot it otherwise there's just random music in your story. You must show at least a smidgen of where it's coming from.

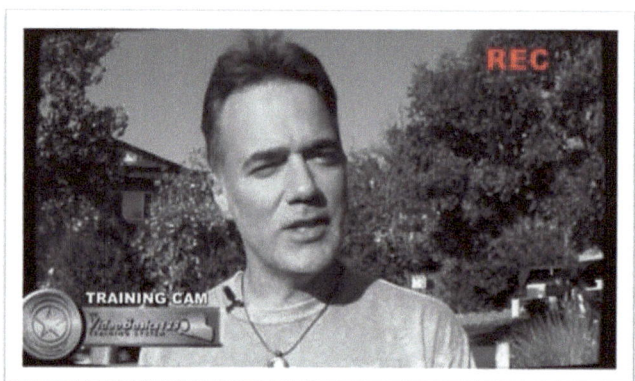

To get natural sound you can't be shy. Sometimes you have to get close. But keep your head on a swivel for other action around you. You must always be ready to capture great video and sound.

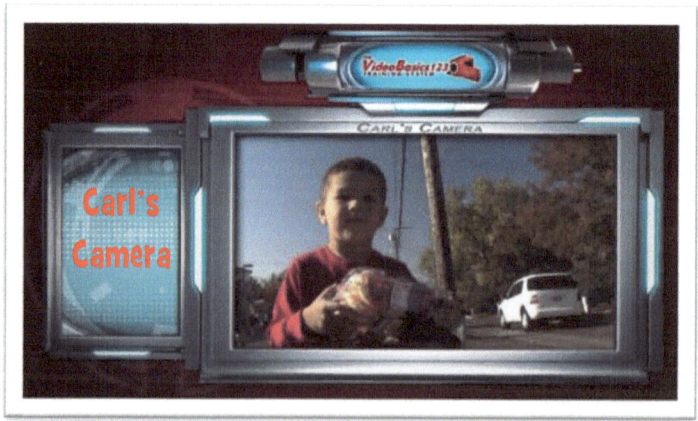

There's usually natural sound, especially at a sporting event.

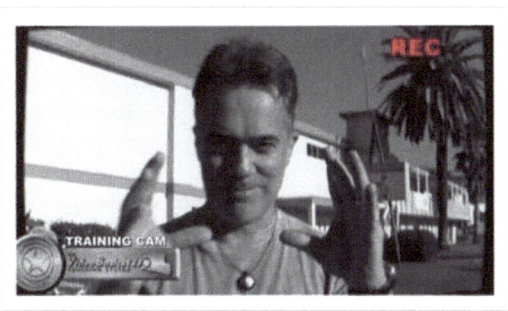

If you are going to hear the sounds of the ball being kicked, you must be close. You can't put a mic on every player out there. So you have to get close enough for the shotgun microphone to pick up great natural sound.

Listen for all the sounds here. Do you hear the kids, parents and the coach?

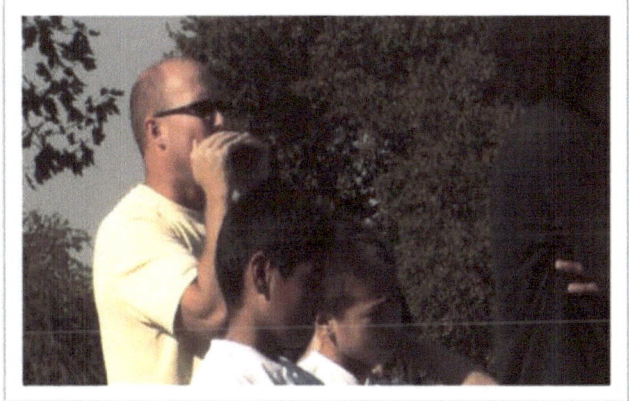

Now there's a coach going bananas. We are going to shoot some of that. We're still pretty far away so I want to get closer so we can hear the coach.

19

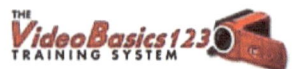

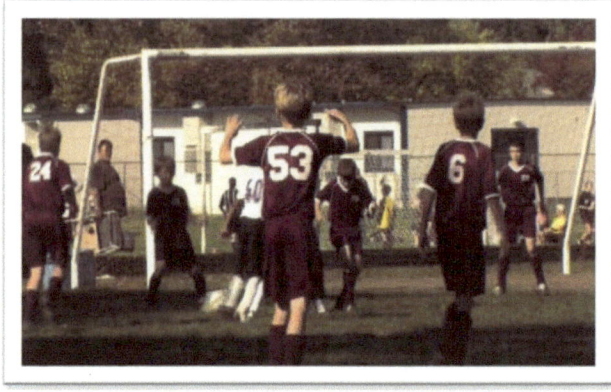

It must be working 'cause the kids are playing hard.

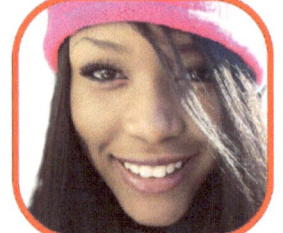

Carl's Assistant: So, here's a quick review. If you're capturing natural sound with a shotgun mic you may have to get close and always wear headphones to make sure you can hear what you're looking at and keep your head on a swivel so you don't miss any great action and sounds.

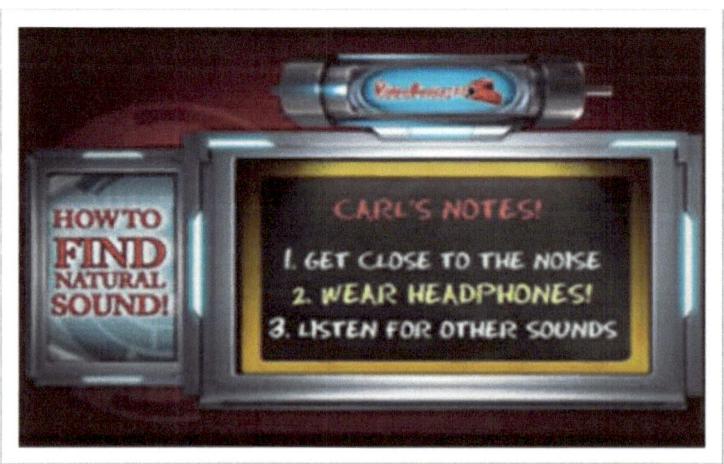

Let's head back to the studio as Carl warms up with a rock and roll band.

Shooting a Small Concert

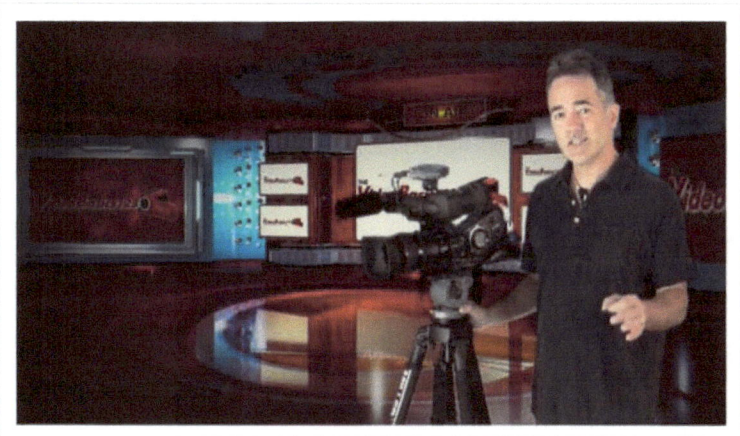

Now let's say you're at an event and you want to get the band. The band is playing up on stage. Don't stand across the street and shoot them. Don't stand right in front of the singer's face and shoot either. Someone in the crowd is going to be like, "Hey, get outta' the way, dude!"

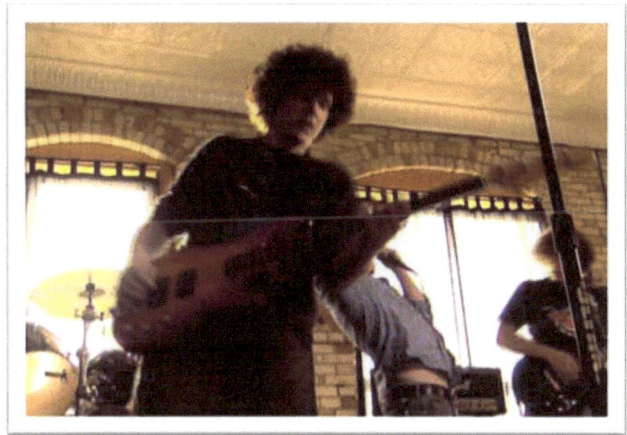

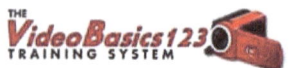

The speakers are going to be probably blaring. The band's pretty loud if I'm guessing my band. So try get to a spot somewhere in the middle. If you're getting bumped a lot you should try to find a spot, maybe a platform, maybe a riser where you can be nice steady.

Once you get settled in make sure that when you're shooting the band you plug your earphones in so can hear them.

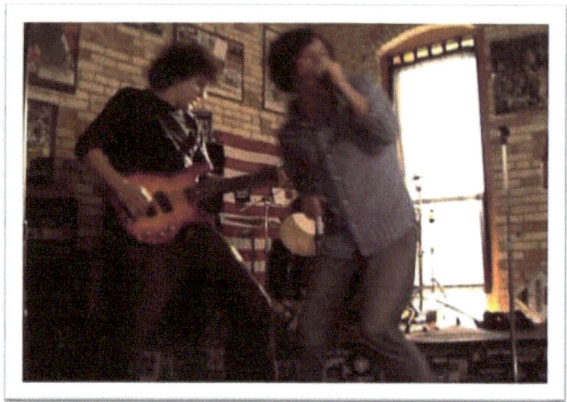

Then adjust your audio because the band is probably going to be loud! Probably so loud that your audio levels are going to be hitting the red. They're going to be too hot. If you have the type of camera that allows you to adjust your audio levels check them often. I'm not going to tell you exactly how to check them because every camera's different. But if there is a feature this is the perfect time to plug your ear and adjust that audio until it's just right. If you really can't hear because the band is so loud, look at your levels. If they're popping way up high, turning red, just one solid line, it's probably too loud.

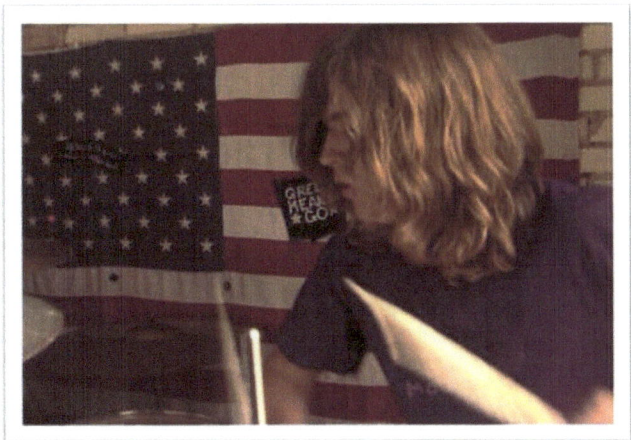

As you're recording the band roll for at least ten seconds. You think, "Oh, that's phenomenal", until you start editing and then you'll see you don't have enough. You want to bring that music underneath your audio in the background and then you quickly learn you didn't record enough music for your story.

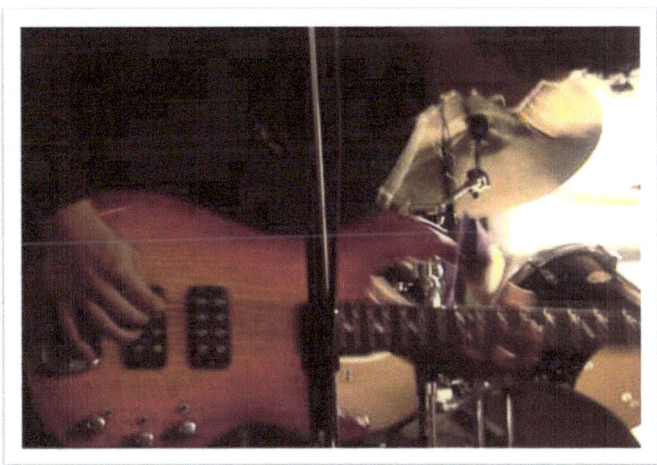

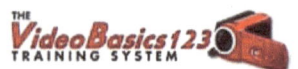

Ten seconds is not going to cut it. You should roll for at least one minute. You're not trying to steal their song, but you do want the sound underneath the interview or underneath the guy telling their story. You may have the music come up for five or six seconds and go back down. If you don't have enough music you won't have many editing options.

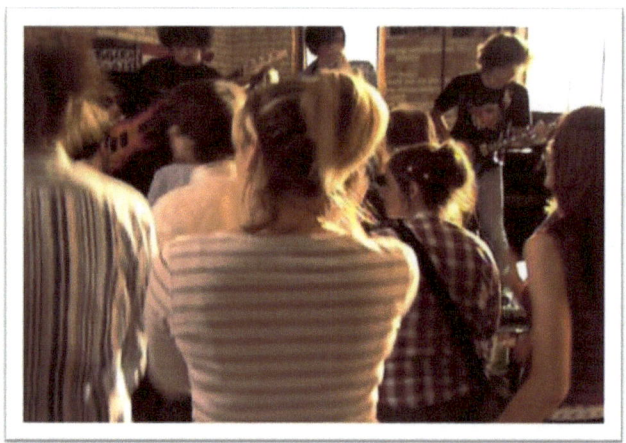

The music part in editing is only for a little bit, but you need to have at least a minute's worth of music so you can edit that later. If you just keep turning the camera off and on it's really hard to get consistent sound throughout your whole story, especially when music's involved.

Carl's Assistant: Shooting a band is a little more complicated, but it's easy if you follow these rules. Watch your distance so you don't get in the way of the band and become a major distraction. And once again, wear your

headphones to make sure you're hearing what you're seeing and shoot one minute of continuous music so you'll have plenty of audio when you edit later.

Also, if you have the type of camcorder where you can check your levels, keep them out of the red. If you don't then you may have to depend on your headphones.

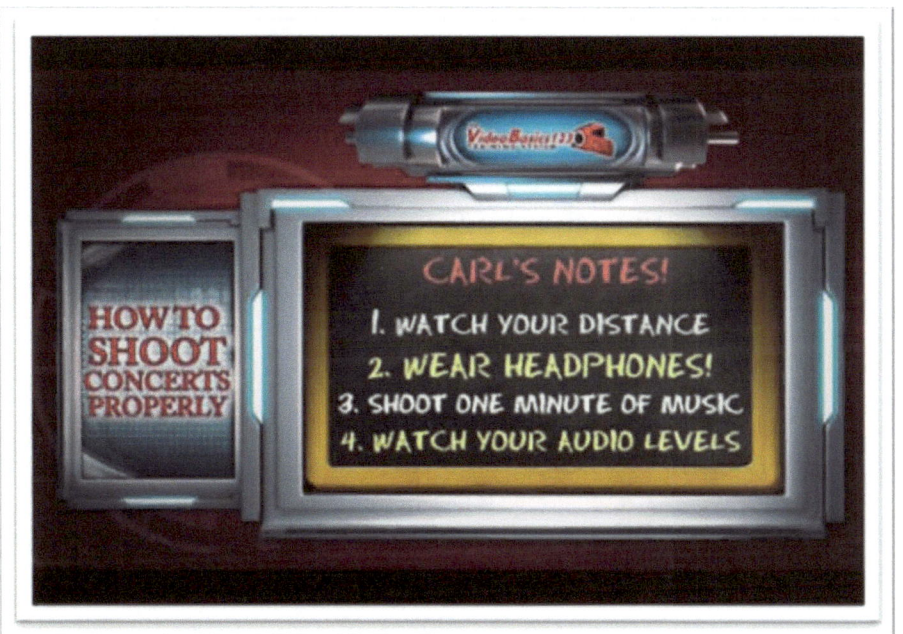

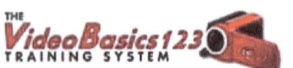

Checking Your Audio before Leaving Event

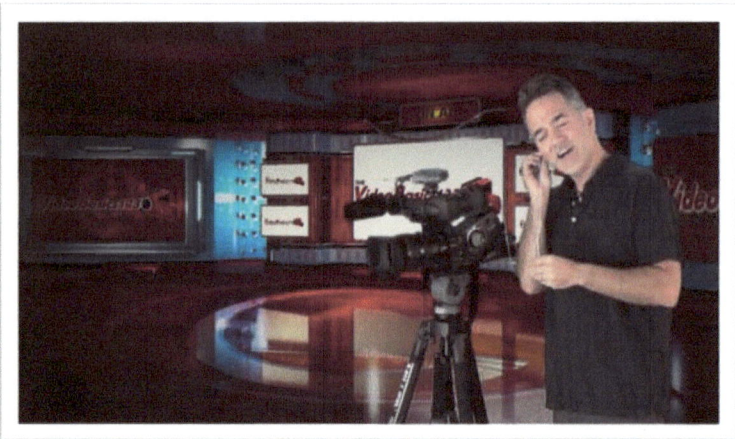

Your day is almost done! You've been shooting. Have you checked your audio lately? I'm pretty sure you've got a tape in the camera, right? Let's check just in case.

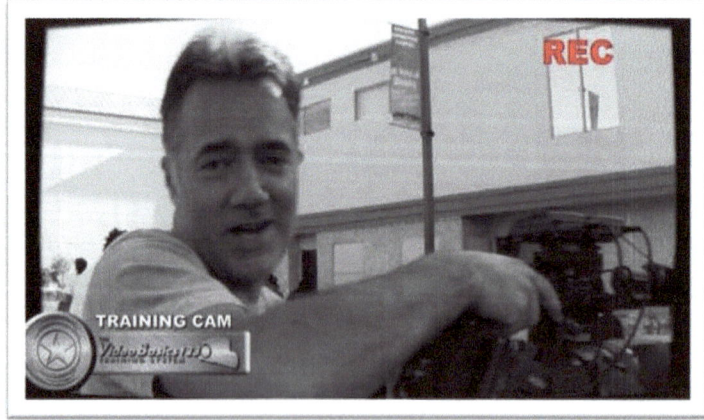

Let's go back. Rewind your tape a little bit or check out your digital card and make sure your earphone is still in and hit play. If necessary go around the corner where it's quitter so you can plug one ear so you can really hear it. You want to make sure that when your subject is talking that there is not a loud car driving by or a plane flying through your shot where all you can hear is an engine revving. Nobody wants to hear that. You can't hear your story, and the guy at home watching is going to wonder what's being said.

Make sure you check your audio before you go home. At some point in your day, make sure it sounds good.

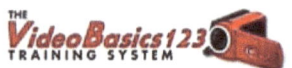

Shooting to Edit!

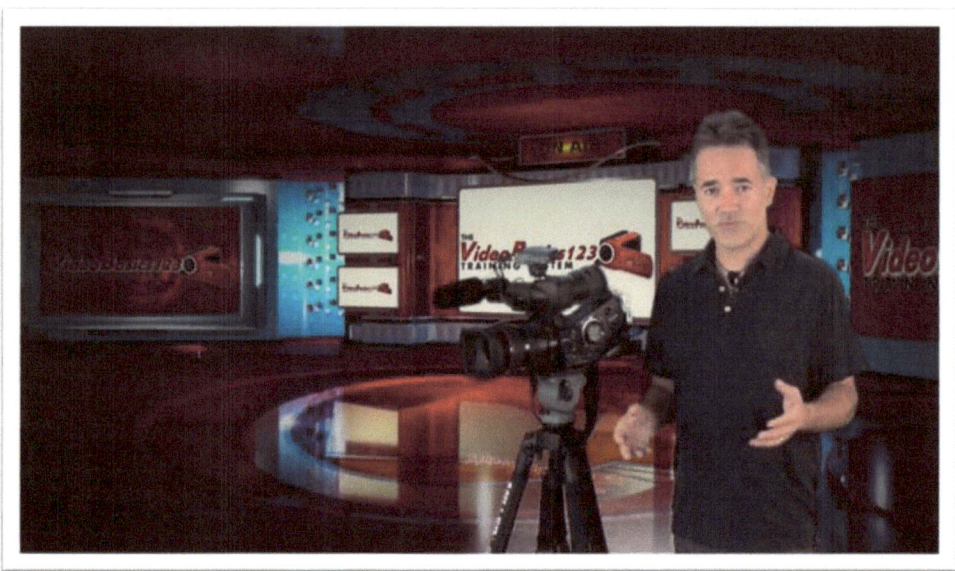

You're about to go out and shoot your video. Have you thought about editing? I mean I know that's after shooting. But if you're shooting to edit this will really help you out.

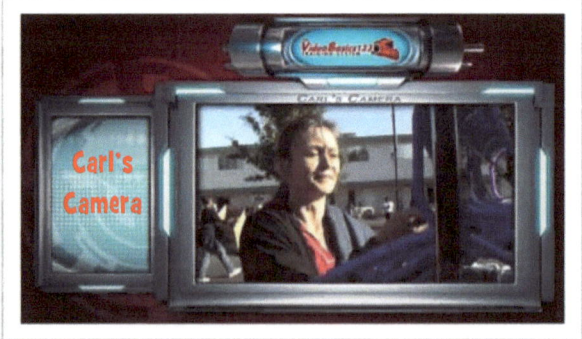

First off, in editing you're going to need a wide shot. So when you're shooting you should shoot a wide shot. In editing you're going to need a medium shot, maybe a tight shot to edit to the wide shot. So when shooting you have to get a wide, a medium and a tight shot.

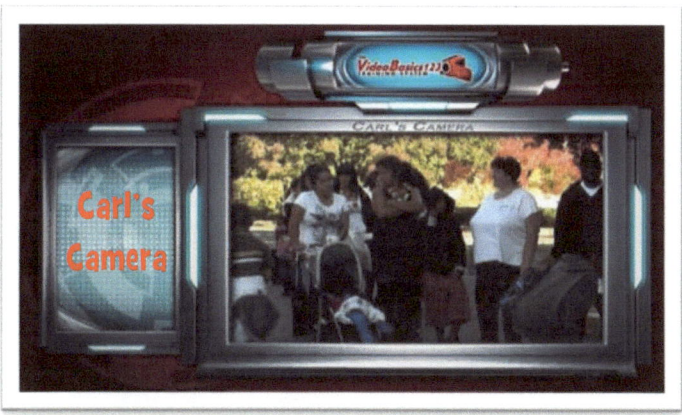

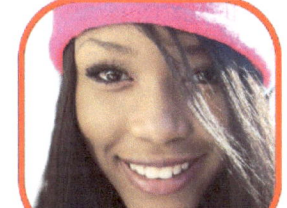**Carl's Assistant:** Let's head out to an event that's helping those in need to see how the wide, medium and tight shots work. Anytime you shoot an event you have to always think in terms of wide, medium, and tight.

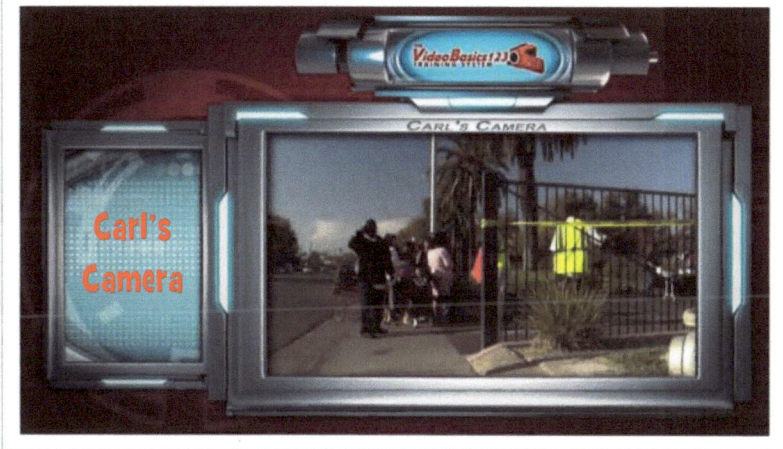

This is a wide shot. It should be one of the first things you shoot. It helps the viewer know where you are

29

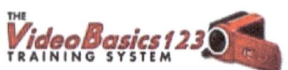

and what's taking place. It helps establish what's going on around you. Carl, the wide shot can be kind of boring, don't you think?

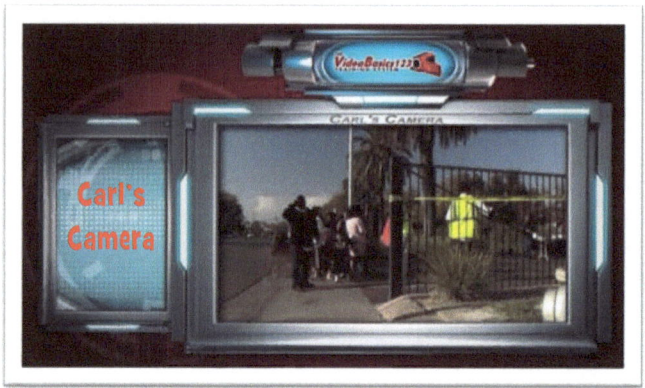

Carl:　　　　　It may seem a little boring, but that wide shot helps me establish where we are and that's just the first wide shot. It's just this scene. There's a lot more to get, a lot more wide shots, a lot more tight shots, a lot more medium shots. It's a good start though.

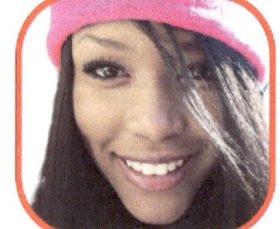

Carl's Assistant: Okay. Now that we know the importance of a wide shot, it's time to zoom in a little closer to the medium shot. As you can see, it takes you closer to the action and gives the viewer an even clearer picture of what's taking place.

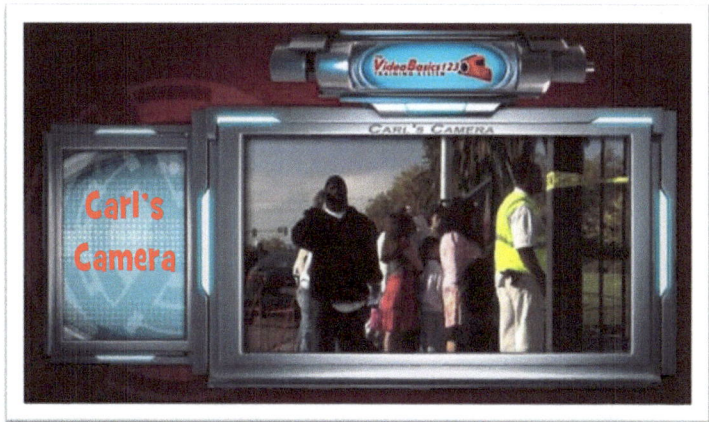

Carl: Yeah! You know what I did? I zoomed in and I got a medium shot. Yeah!

Carl's Assistant: Now Carl is adjusting his focus so he can get a tight shot. A tight shot brings you even closer to the action so you can see more details like facial expressions.

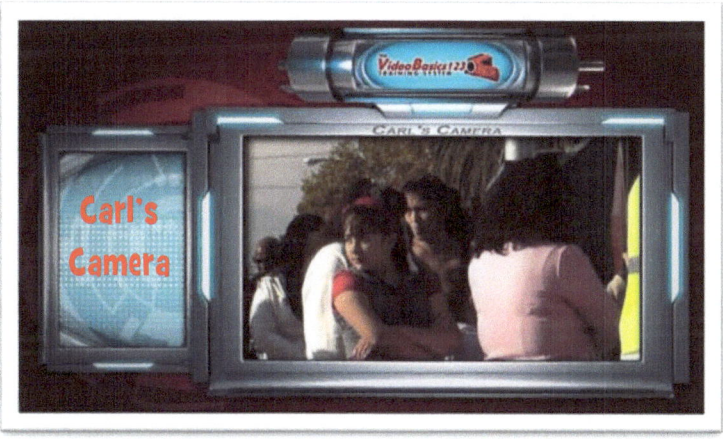

Carl: Anyone? Anyone? Yeah! Tight shot. Okay. Let's move closer to the action.

31

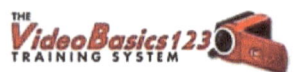

Carl's Assistant: Carl is now getting closer to the action. You have to be careful because he's shooting from the street. He's once again shooting a wide shot to show the viewer that people are standing in line.

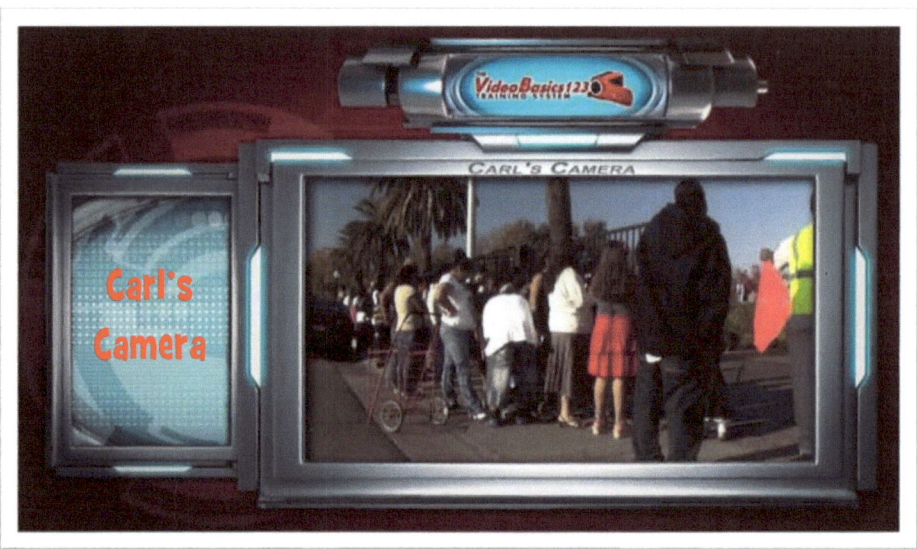

Carl:

This is also kind of a wide shot with a pan by tuning the camera from left to right only because I couldn't squeeze it all in. I don't like to do pans and zooms very often, but I can't stand in the street and shoot this, so I just panned the camera from left to right a little bit to show everything.

Let's have some fun. Remember, if you don't shoot perfectly just try again. Don't be afraid to shoot your shot twice. It's just tape or a digital card. If you mess it up, you can always do it again, right?

Carl's Assistant: **Now Carl is trying his low angle wide shot.**

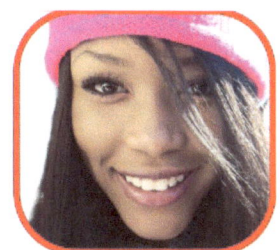

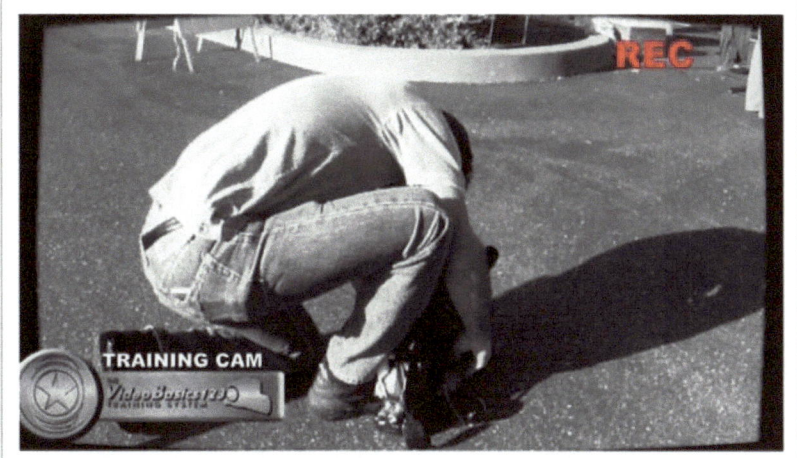

Now as you can see I look kind of goofy way down here, but the shot looks good. I can see the word cloths. I can see people and yes, it's a wide shot.

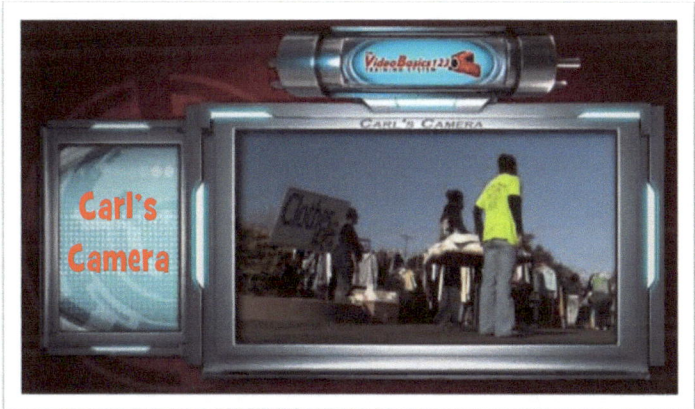

Now you may be thinking, enough with the wide shots already. But did you know that these wide shots are an editor's best friend? I know I get kind of crazy with the

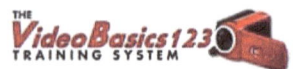

wide shots and all, but trust me. You can see a lot more in this shot so why not, right. It's just tape.

Carl's Assistant: Watch as Carl goes from a wide shot to show what's about to happen and then he walks up close to get a tight shot of a ticket being punched.

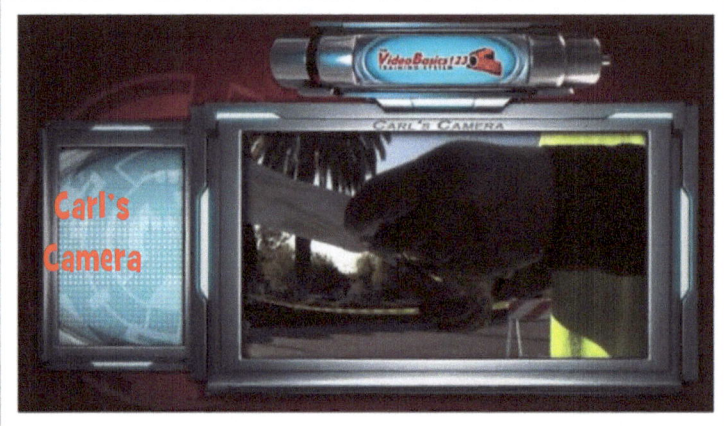

As an editor this gives him a lot more material to work with.

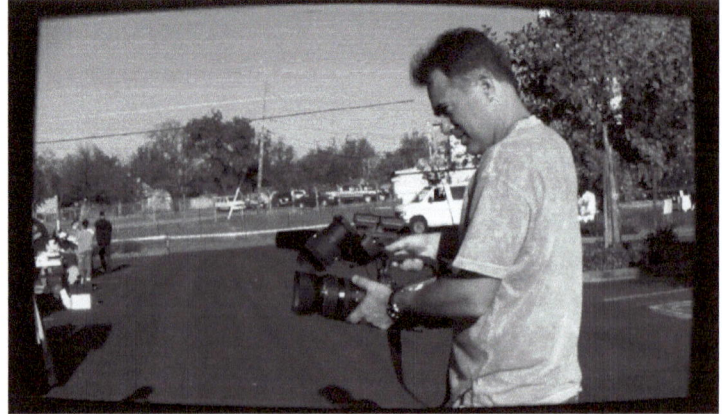

I've got some natural sound of the tickets. Then I got a wide shot, something I can edit too. There's a ticket being punch right there, so I got a tight shot of that. Now let's get a wide shot.

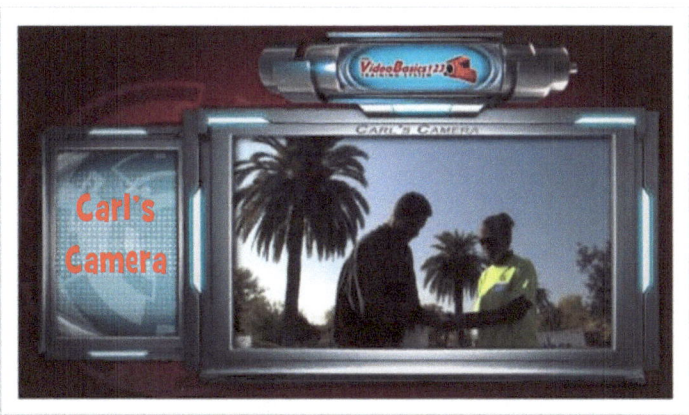

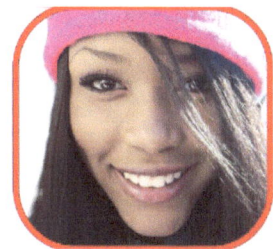 There's so many shots to consider, but if you stick with the principles of wide, medium and tight it'll make sure you're editing is a lot easier. Let's sit back and watch cameraman Carl work.

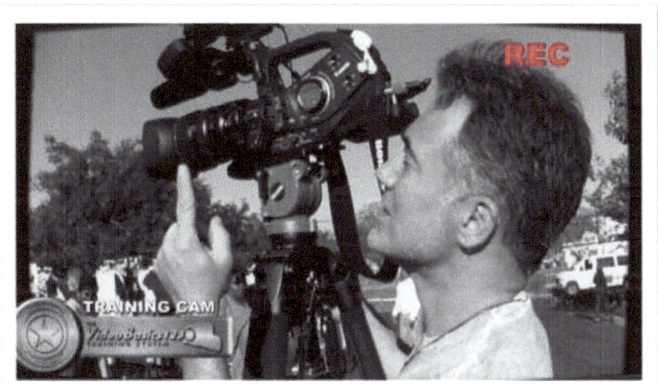

One thing I do a lot when I'm shooting is I very quietly say one, two, three, four, five, six. That way I know I've got a nice solid five-second shot that I can use. I don't'

35

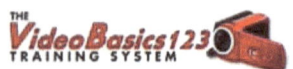

say it loudly because again, microphone is right there. It can hear me!

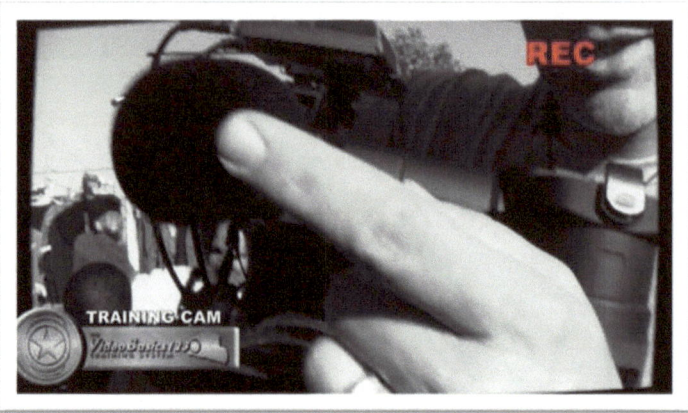

Watch. I'm going to set my shot up here, zoom in, hit record, then go –

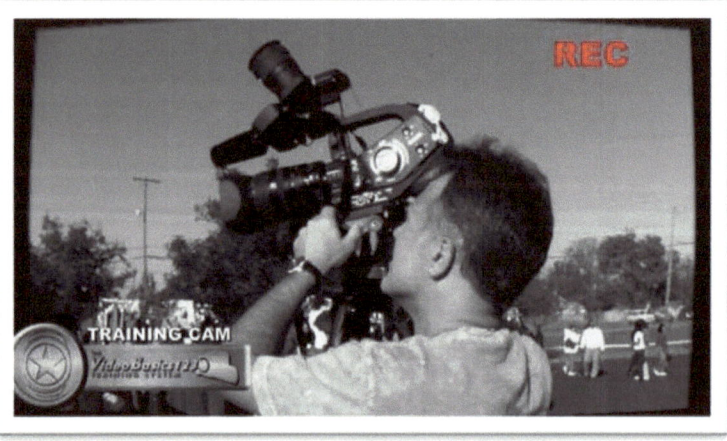

One, two, three, four, five, six, seven. I've got plenty to edit with now. This is great!

We've got some people shopping. Let's get some video of what they're shopping for. Just some dresses. They're kind of boring static shots, but we'll get a couple shots of dresses and a few more shots of shoppers. We don't know how much we're going to need. There is no script yet. So we shoot a little more than we think we're going to need and then we shoot even more.

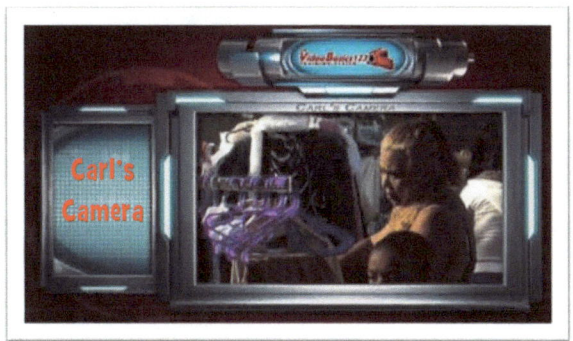

Alright. Let's go a little crazy. We're going to do a walk through with the camera on my shoulders just to see what happens. When I do a walk through I keep my camera focus wide and walk at a brisk pace. This helps put the viewer in the moment. It's a really cool shot!

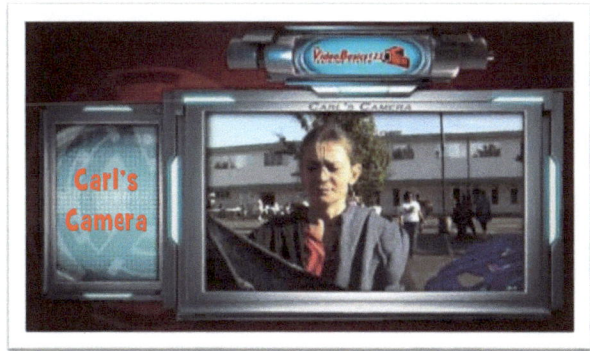

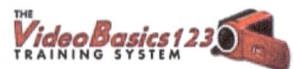

Carl's Assistant: Now Carl has moved to the food giveaway where the same principles apply; wide, medium and tight.

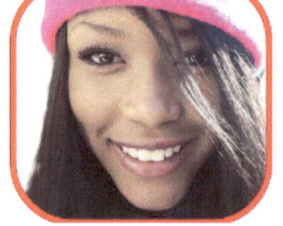

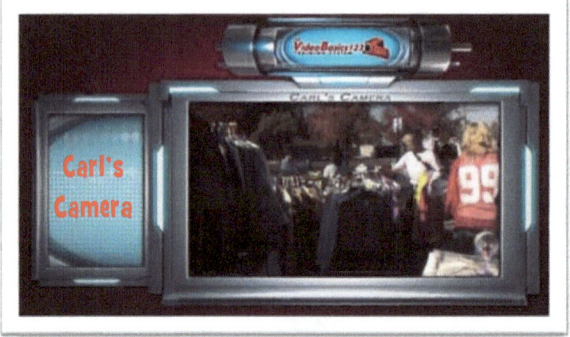

Carl: If I'm in the middle of getting one of my famous medium shots and things change, like they walk out of the shot. Well, I just pretend I didn't get that shot and move on to another. You can't use that empty. You didn't get it! So make sure you just keep shooting until you get the shot you want.

Carl's Assistant: Okay. It's time to take a shooting quiz. Can you identify the following shots? Do your best.

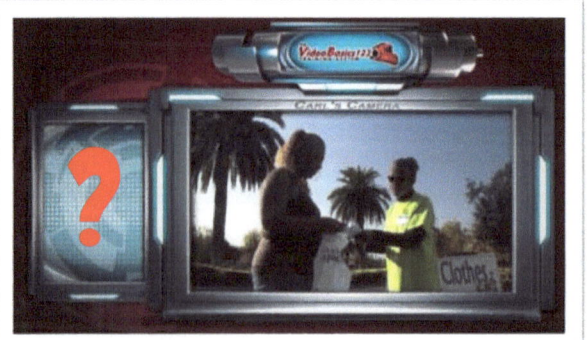

If you guessed medium shot, you're right. Let's go to the next one.

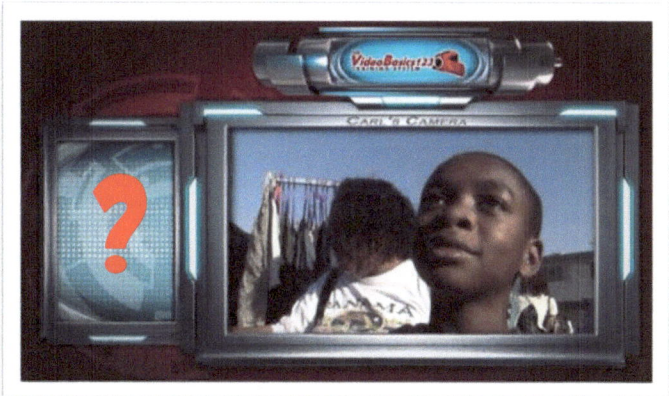

Of course. It's a tight shot. It's a close-up and shows more detail. Let's move on.

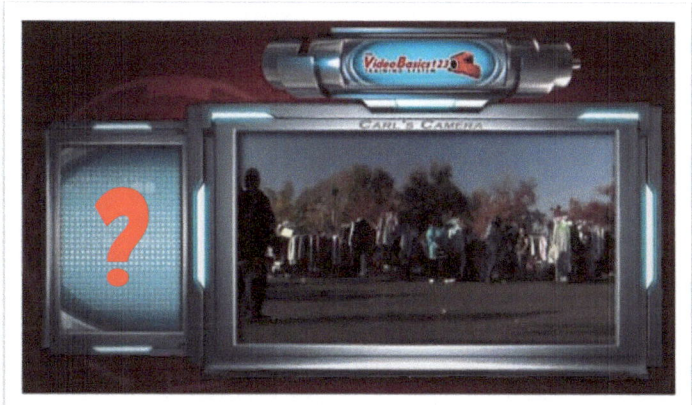

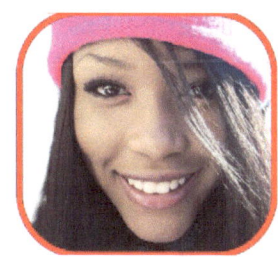 **I think this one was too easy. If you guessed wide shot you guessed correctly. Let's wrap things up in the studio.**

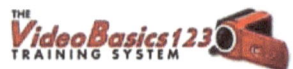

Carl: So remember, in editing you're going to need a wide shot. When you're shooting you should shoot a wide shot and in editing you're going to need a medium shot, maybe a tight shot to edit to the wide shot. So when shooting you have to get a wide, a medium and a tight.

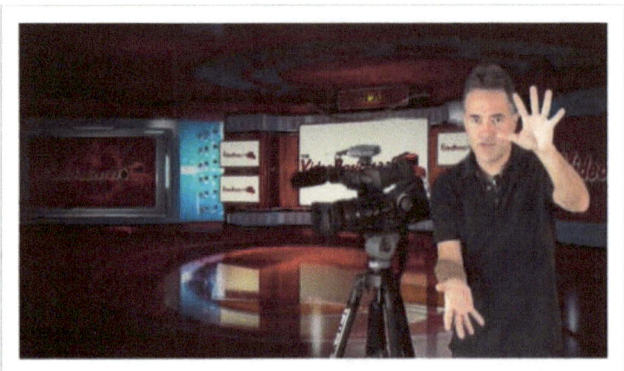

What does that mean exactly? If you're shooting a band, for example, get the wide shot. Trust me on this. It's the same as if I walk into a room. My eyes automatically adjust to the room. In a split second I take in a wide shot. Then I kind of glance over at something else for more of a medium shot. Then I might glance over and I focus in to a tight shot. I'm not dizzy. I'm not lost. I'm just doing what my eyes naturally do when walking into a room.

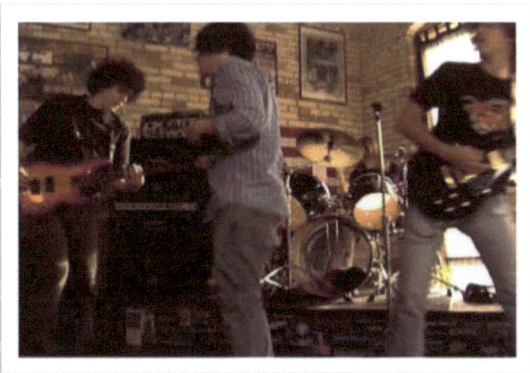

You want to mimic that! You want to pretend that this camera is doing the same thing your eyes do automatically and that is getting a wide shot, getting a medium shot and getting a tight shot. If I could tell you this five times in a row I would. Well I could, but I won't. You could just rewind it five times and play it again and again and again.

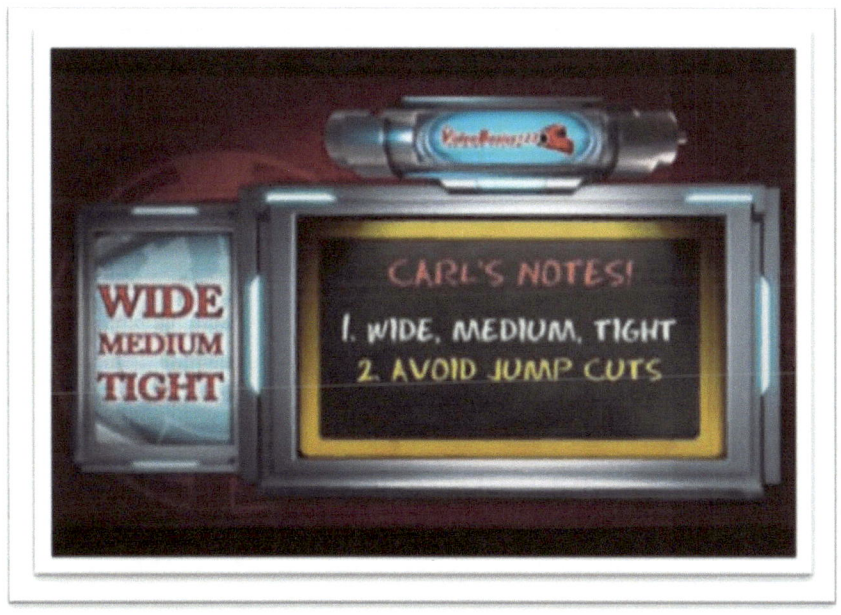

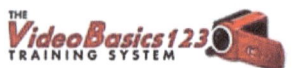

Basic Outdoor Lighting Techniques

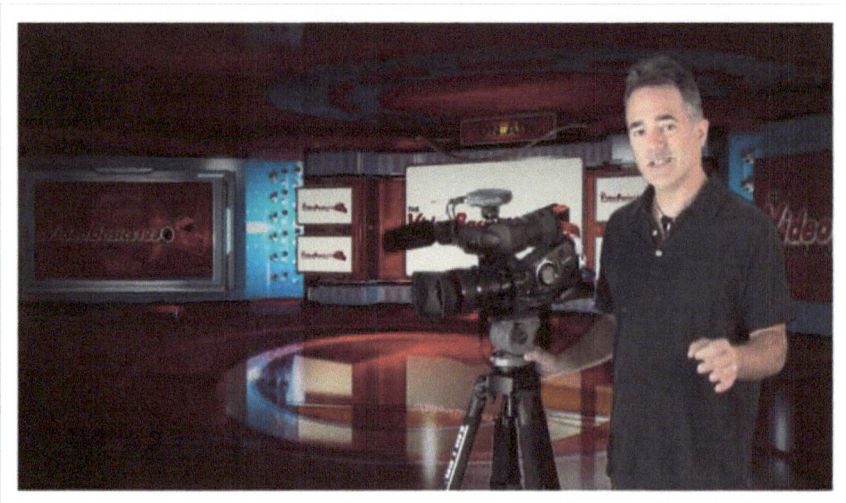

Let's talk about lighting. If you can't see what you're shooting, I don't know why you're even there because you have to be bale see it to shoot it.

You may or may not have a light on top of your camera. You may or may not have fancy lights. We're using some really fancy lights right now. I should look fantastic right now.

Anyway, you must have light. So let's for just a minute say you don't even have a flashlight. I recommend shooting in daylight!

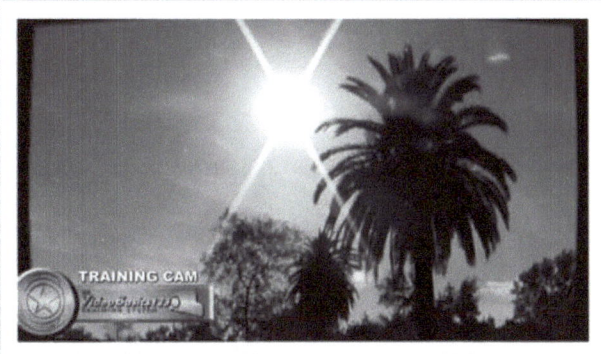

Let's assume that you don't have any lights, but the event you are shooting is outside. You've got one great big light in the sky. I call it the sun. It works fantastic, so let's use that.

Where do you position yourself so the sun works for you? You don't want your interviewee squinting because of the sun is right there. He's going to go blind!

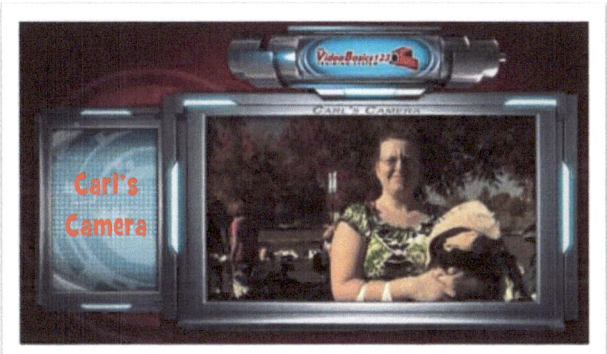

Instead you want to turn the subject slightly. You want the light to hit one side of his face with a little shadow here or the other side with a little shadow.

43

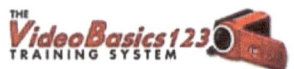

Why create a little shadow at all? Well, if he has just straight light on him, aside from possibly going blind, his features will all meld into one very flat image. If you create a little bit of shadow on the back of his face, regardless of the direction he's facing, make sure it's the backside of his face. That creates a 3D effect.

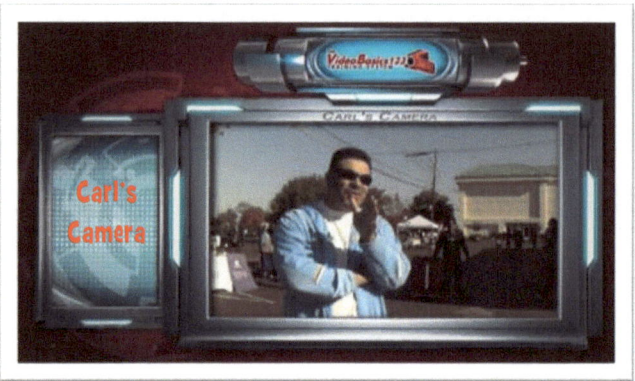

I repeat use the sun. If the sun is over here you're going to position your subject dead on and then turn him 25 degrees this way or this way. He's still looking into the sun a little bit, but not straight on.

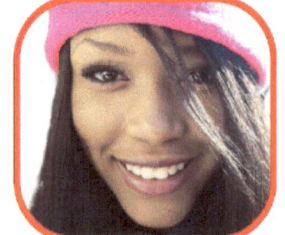

Carl's Assistant: Here's some great examples. There are a lot of things to consider when shooting outdoors, such as the time of day and the weather conditions. But as Carl pointed out, if you use the sun to light only a portion of the face it makes the person look more three-dimensional.

Skin tone and color can be factors, too.

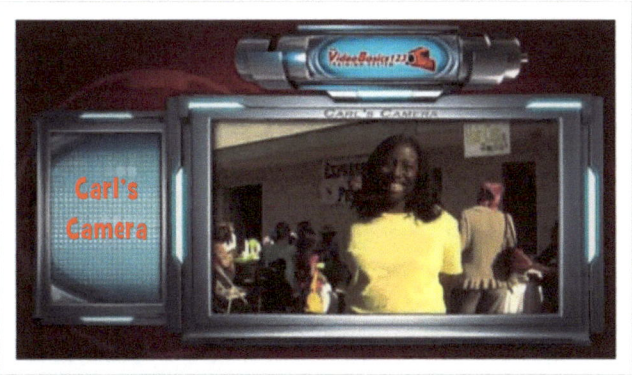

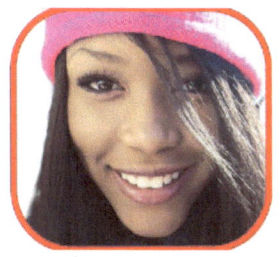

Remember, the sun can be your best friend·or worst enemy. It all depends on how you use it. Here's Carl to break it down.

Carl: When it comes to the sun, you can't shoot directly into it, nor can you shoot directly behind it either. If you shoot directly into it, the sun can flare your lens and create a big white spot. Behind it, the subjects turn into shadows. But from these weird angles, like 45 degree angle over my shoulder is good. You can see if it looks good, right?

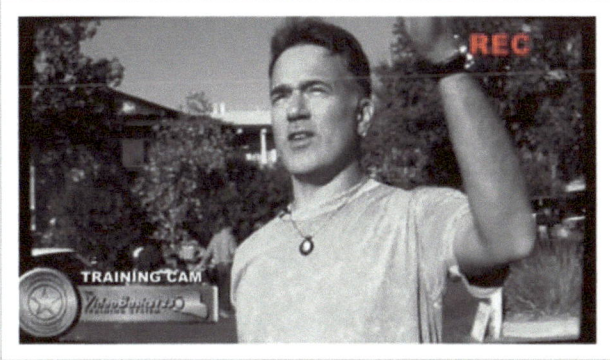

45

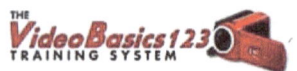

Carl's Assistant: Let's head back to the studio for more lighting tips.

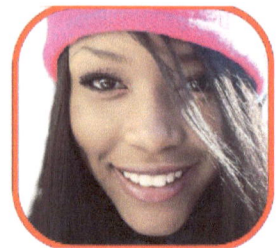

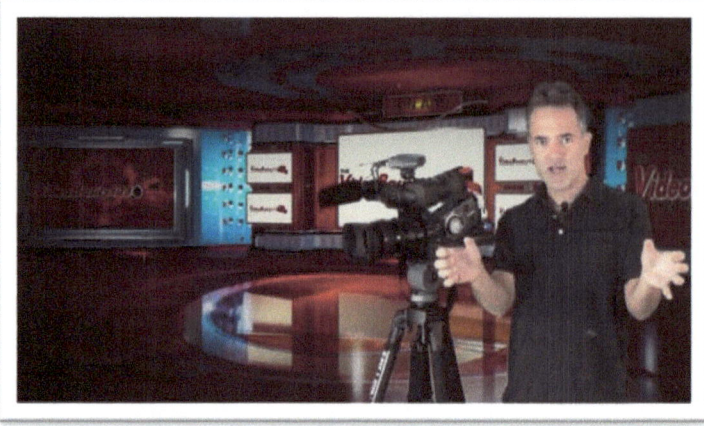

Carl: When shooting your event you probably have no choice on the time of day you shoot, but noon is a lousy time of day to shoot. The sun is straight up ahead and almost anywhere you stand the shadows come right down your eyes.

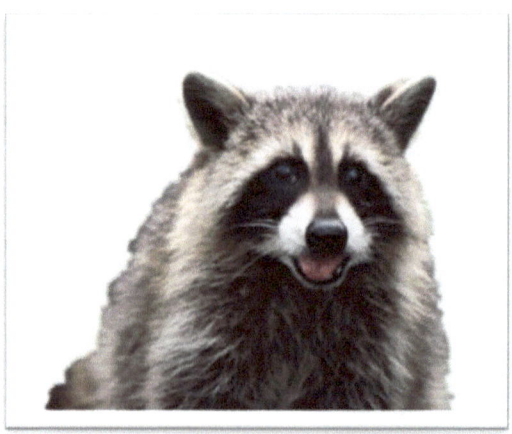

We call them raccoon eyes. It looks awful! You either need to pull your subject aside into the shade, pull them somewhere away from the sun, or put the sun behind them so there's shadow all in front of their face.

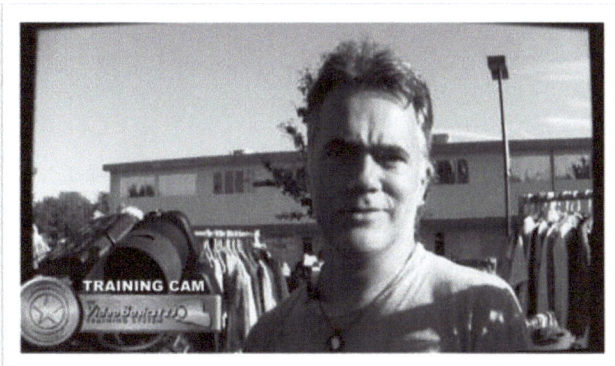

Now there's a lot of pitfalls here because if you have the sun behind your subject, their face may be too dark. If you have the white-hot sky behind them, I guarantee you won't see their face. So find a dark background, such as some trees, a building or something to put behind them so you can see their face.

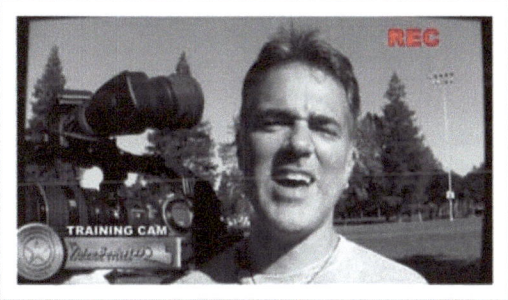

The most important thing in your interview shot is lighting the entire face when you're shooting.

47

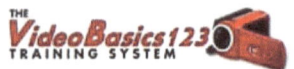

If you're lucky enough to shoot when the sun is setting, you must shoot really fast because that sun is changing really fast. As beautiful as it is, you may get a beautiful shot. Then five minutes later you may be standing in pitch darkness. So shoot fast if you're shooting at sunset.

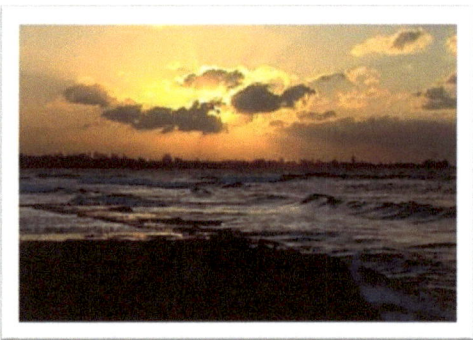

Plus, if you're shooting five or six shots at sunset this shot may not match the next shot. Even though they're only two minutes apart, your lighting, the sun is going down so fast it's changing your shots.

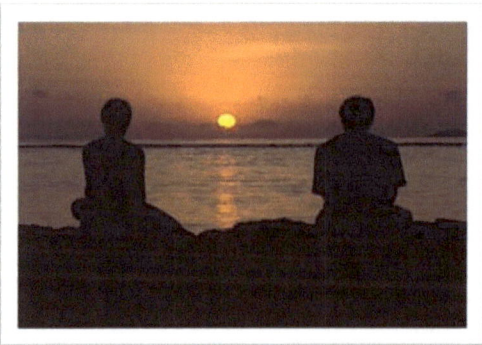

Carl's Assistant: Once again, light only a portion of the face on a sunny day. Try to avoid raccoon eyes and remember how the light can quickly change at sunset.

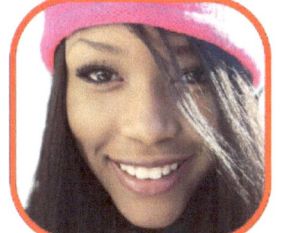

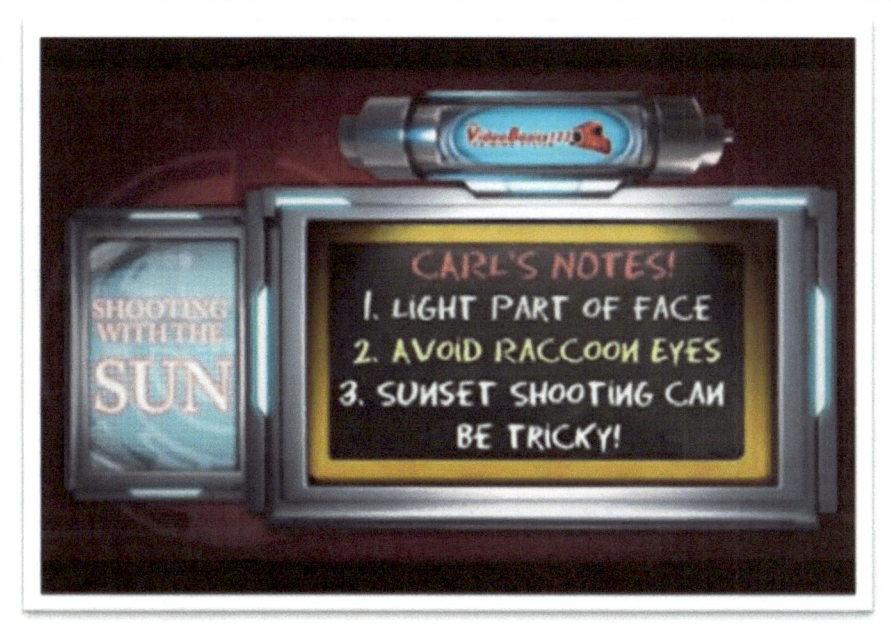

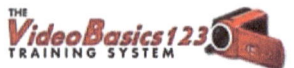

Why Use a Tripod?

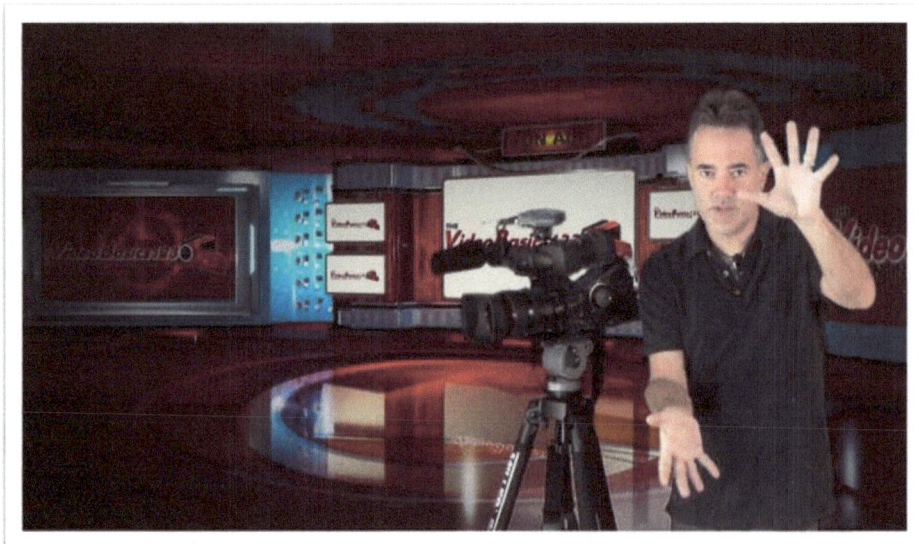

If you're out there, getting great shots, but you don't have a tripod, it's a whole different way of shooting. If you don't have a tripod, make sure you get close because if you step way back and then zoom way in, chances are no matter how steady you think you are it's going to look awful. It's going to be like an earthquake.

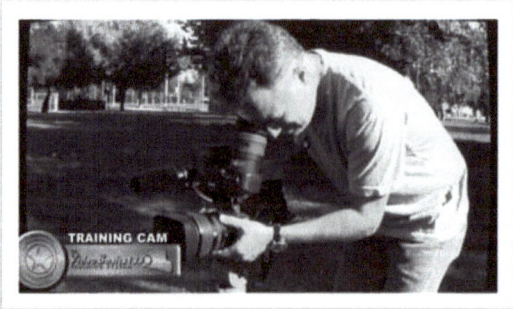

If you can get a tripod that's pretty good because tripods works great. If you don't have a tripod, then zoom out and walk up to your subject nice and close. It's much steadier. Because as soon as you zoom in and you're far away while shooting chances are you're going to make somebody throw up.

Carl's Assistant: **Carl hits the streets to show you why using a tripod is important to keep your shots steady.**

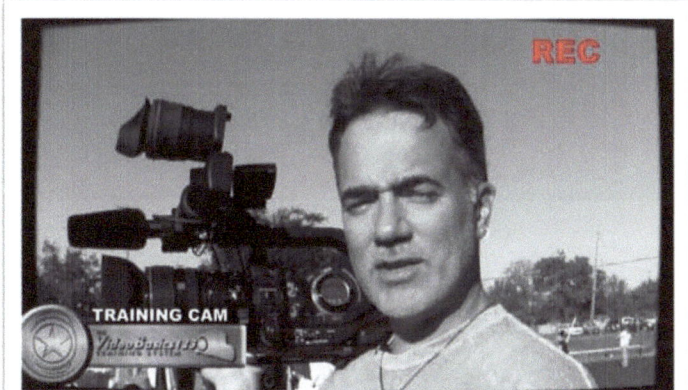

Carl: Okay. I'm going to give you a don't, as in do not do this! I'm pretty far away from the action, but I'm just going to go handheld here, no tripod and zoom in and see what we get.

I'm zooming in and I'm trying to keep it steady, but it's really shaky. For one, this shot is incredibly shaky, two, I can't hear a thing they're saying and I do not want to see this shot in our story. It's just not good. Don't do it!

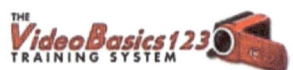

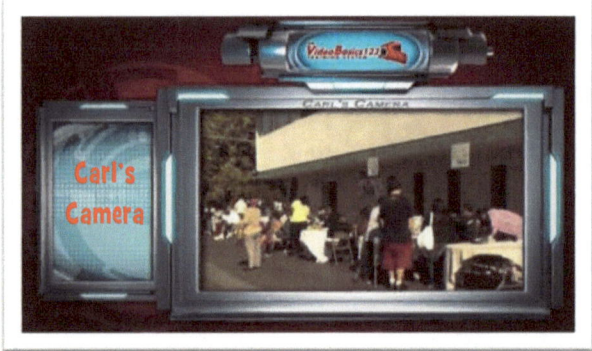

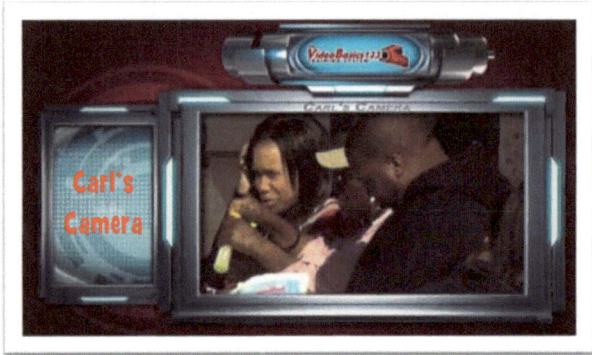

Carl's Assistant: Remember to use a tripod for shots that are far away or focus wide if you don't have a tripod. It's the best way to keep your shots steady.

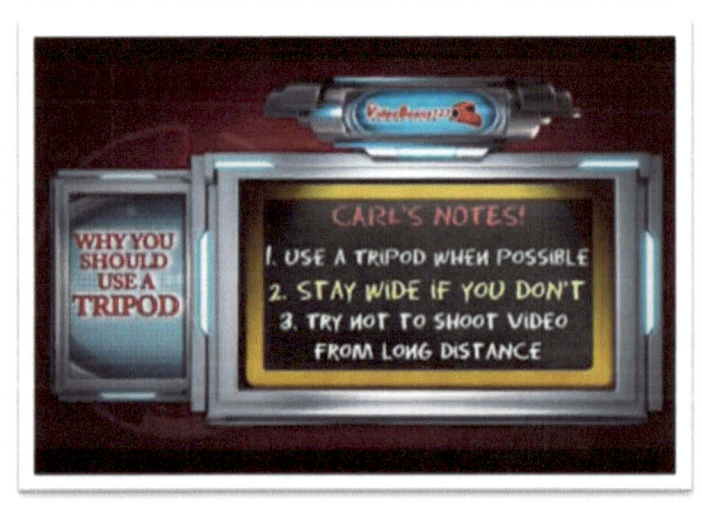

Plan Your Shoot

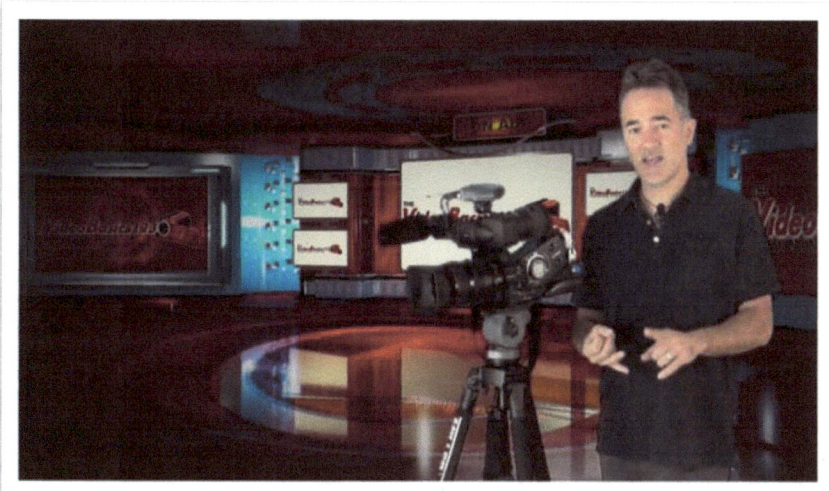

When you're going into editing, plan ahead and think about how you may need a shot for your graphics or a shot for the ending scene or a shot for when the title comes up or when the credits roll. Try to plan out every potential shot you might need.

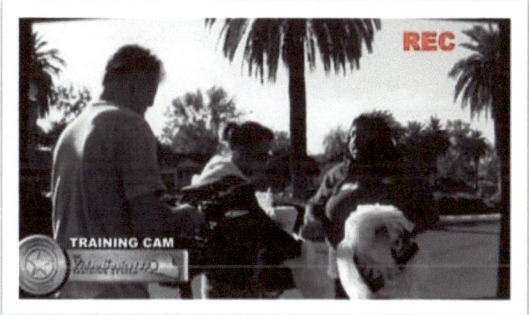

Obviously you're going to get the interviews, shoot the B-roll of the band and you're going to get the wide, medium, tight shots. You might want to think about

53

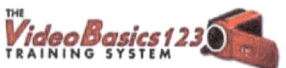

shooting reaction shots of the crowd watching the band. This gives you something extra to edit.

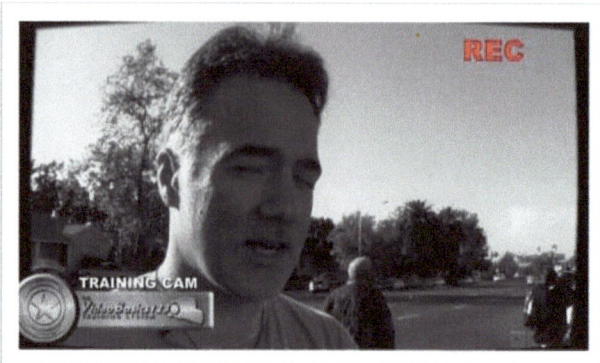

All these extra shots will save you in editing. We will not discuss how to edit. There are so many programs out there. It would take forever to go through every single program and describe the green button versus the red button and the blue button.

However, your story will tell you how to edit. A good example would be editing a rock and roll band. The music may have a fast and upbeat tempo and your edits should be the same.

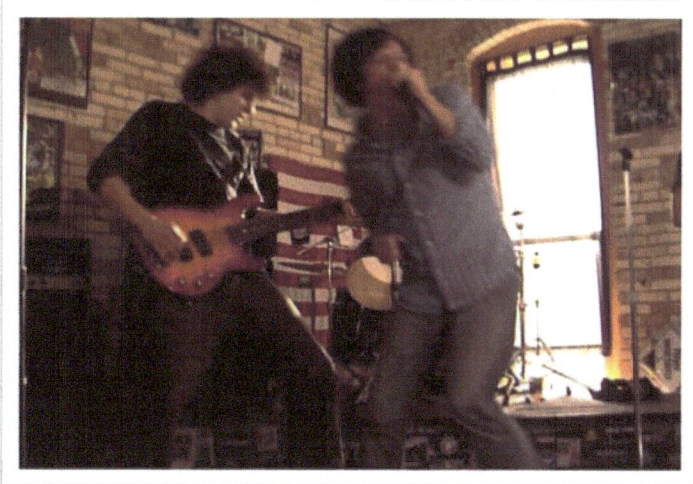

Here's the band playing. Here's the reaction, the kids screaming, the guitar solo. It will work out great. A lot of fast shots.

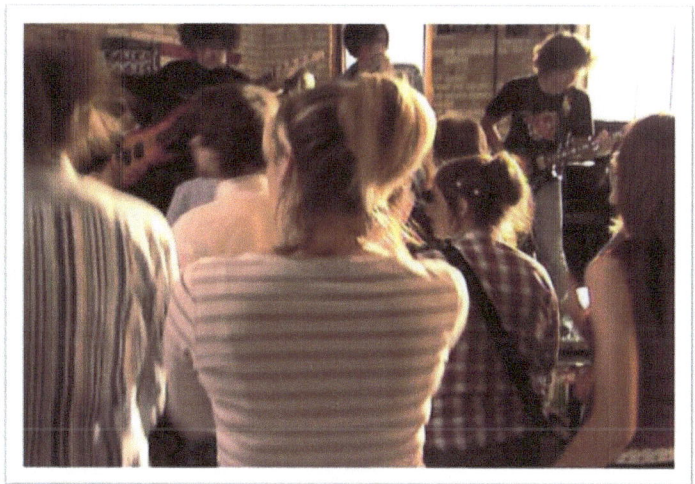

On the contrary if you're at a city council meeting you're probably going to have longer shots of the audience and longer shots of the Mayor or City Councilmembers. It's

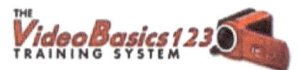

a slower paced story so the shots will probably be edited a little bit longer too.

Carl's Assistant: 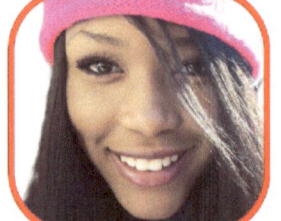 **If you want to make your editing so much easier you should always plan your shoots. It will help determine how many videotapes or cards you need.**

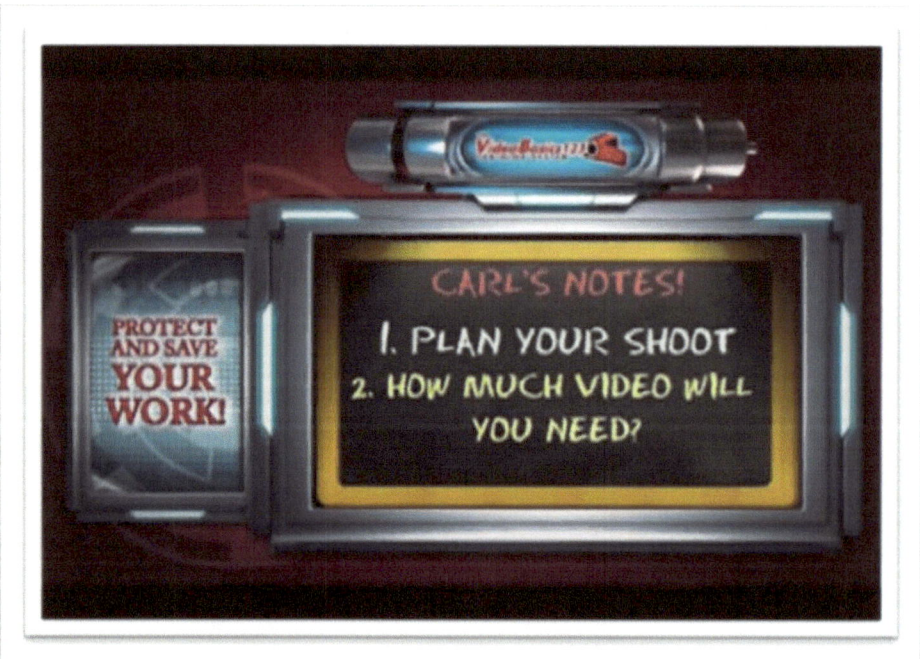

Save It or Loose It!

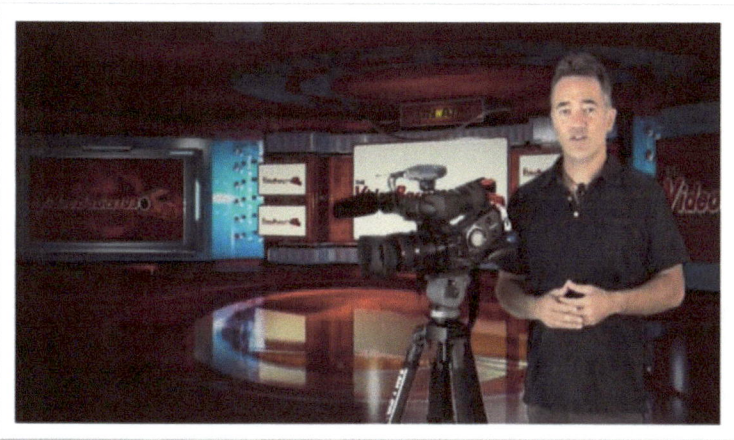

Your shooting day is all done! Now you're ready to edit. Here's something you might want to think about before you actually start editing. If you have a tape, there's a little save tab on it. Go ahead and pop to save it so that way you won't erase your hard work by accident.

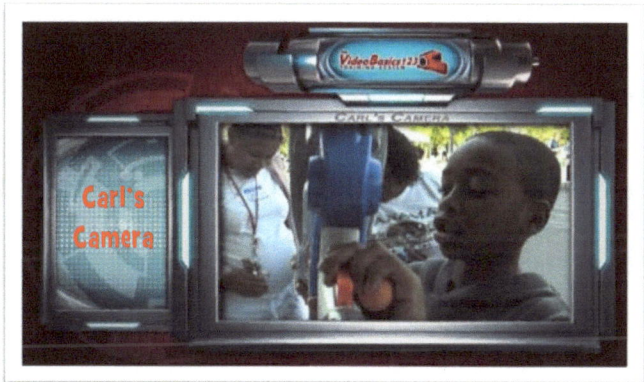

If you have a digital card you want to get that into your computer and onto your hard drive or wherever you're going to put it to make sure it's saved properly and

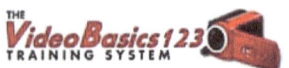

labeled properly. Does it need a name and a date? Are there a lot of other tapes or cards sitting around? Make sure that they are in order so you can find them when editing. Believe me I've been there. It's not a good feeling. It's awful!

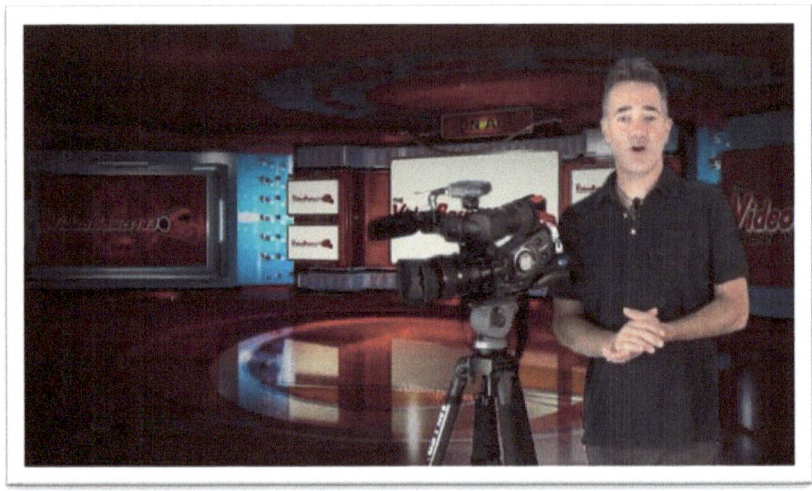

Carl's Assistant: Remember to protect your video. It would be horrible to lose all your hard work and the more organized you are, the easier it will be to edit.

Carl: Finally you've been editing. It's looking fantastic. You're going to go celebrate tonight. Walk away from your computer. Have a good time.   Did you save it? You saved your work. You actually hit save picked a folder and placed it there right? Please tell me you saved it.

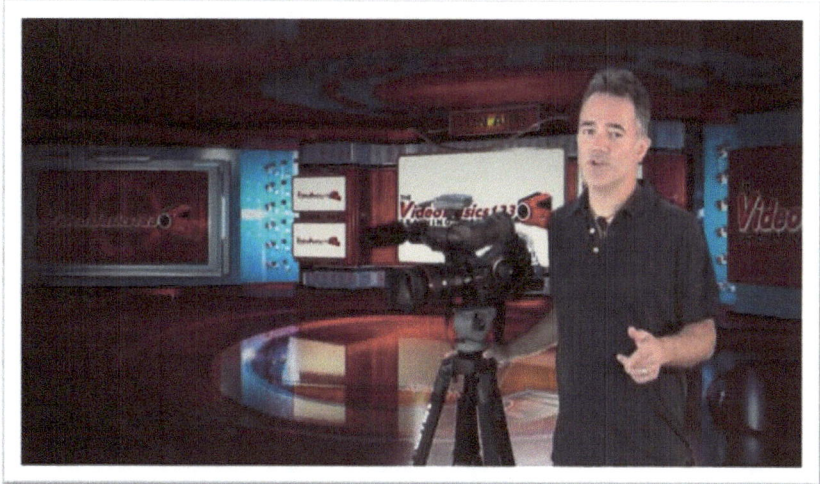

Save your work. As a matter of fact, save it while you're editing. As soon as you load your video, save your work. As you make your first edit, save your work. As you make your fifth edit, save your work. Maybe your program has an automatic save feature; maybe it doesn't. Save your work! Do it yourself. If you're going to get up and grab something to drink, save your work.

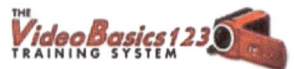

Carl's Assistant: **Remember to save your work before, during and after editing. There's nothing worse than losing all your hard work.**

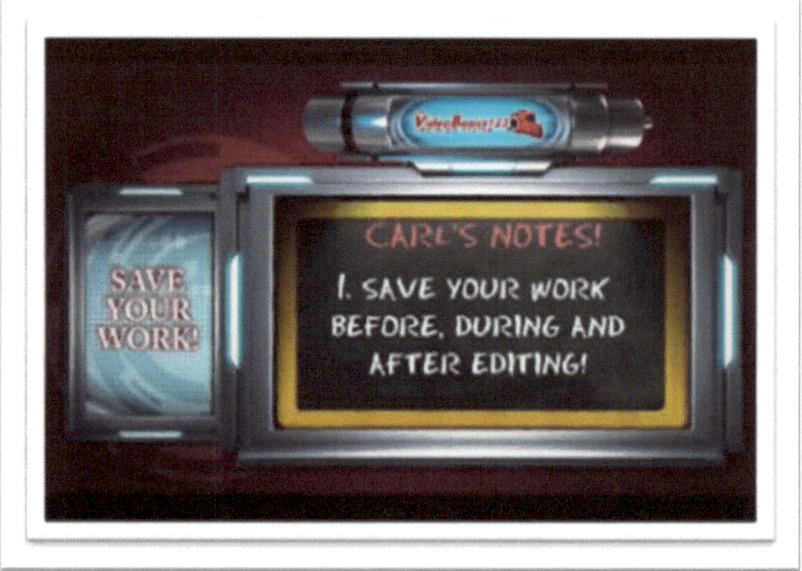

Carl: The next day you come back to your project. You've had a whole night to sleep on it and your buddy says, "Hey, what about that shot of Carrot Top that you got? Oh, you got to put Carrot Top in your piece, dude. You don't see him every day."

No problem because you saved your work! Just open it back up. Find that great shot of Carrot Top, put him in and then save your work again. This is why you save your work. so you don't lose your work.

You're going to make changes. You might even make different versions for different people. You see, Uncle John doesn't' necessarily like Aunt Susie, but they're both in your story. Uncle John wants his own copy. For his version you've got to cut Aunt Susie out and for Aunt Susie's version you've got to cut Uncle John out.

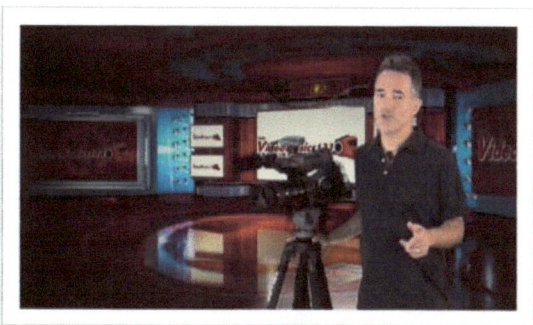

You can make different versions really easily as long as you save it.

So thank you for saving your work. I do appreciate it. But just in case, did you make a movie out of it as well?

You think you're done? Go ahead and make it into a Quick Time movie or a Windows movie. It doesn't really matter what format you choose, but make it into a movie and store that movie somewhere else. If something does happen to your project you've also got a back-up of your project in a movie.

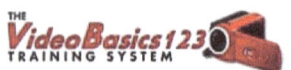

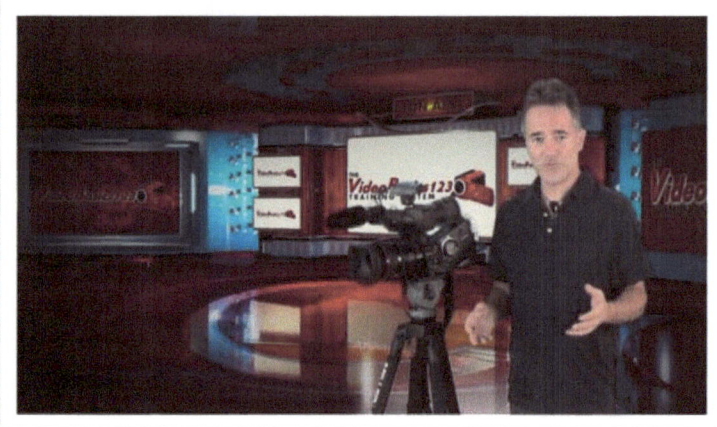

Carl's Assistant: It's always a great idea to make a digital copy of your video whether it's on DVD or as a digital movie. Let's head back to the studio for more life saving tips.

Okay. You saved it. You've made a movie out of it and you're going to premier it next week at your big festival.

You might want to put it on DVD and play it on your TV set because it looks great on your computer, which is not that big, but will it look great on your TV which is a little bit bigger. When you actually see your finished product on TV you might see it's out of focus.

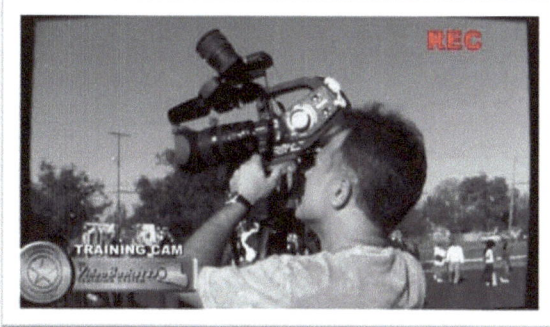

When it's big on the computer screen it doesn't look out of focus. But when it's expanded on a television screen it might look out of focus or you might catch something you never even knew happened. You might see a flash frame. You may say, "Uncle Sean, was that him?" It's one split second some guy just popping into your video.

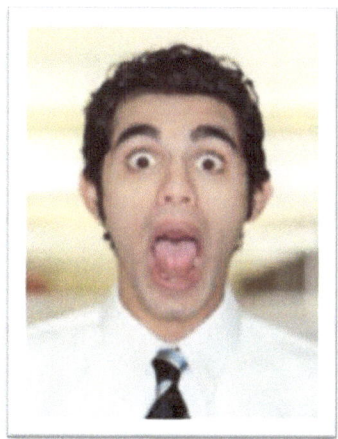

You never know what you're going to find on your new creation that you won't see on your computer but will see on your TV. So before the big premier, put it on a DVD, take it out to the living room and just sit down and watch it. You might find your audio levels are a little

63

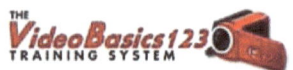

weird. The band is too loud, the interview is too quiet.
Now you can go back and fix it because you saved it.

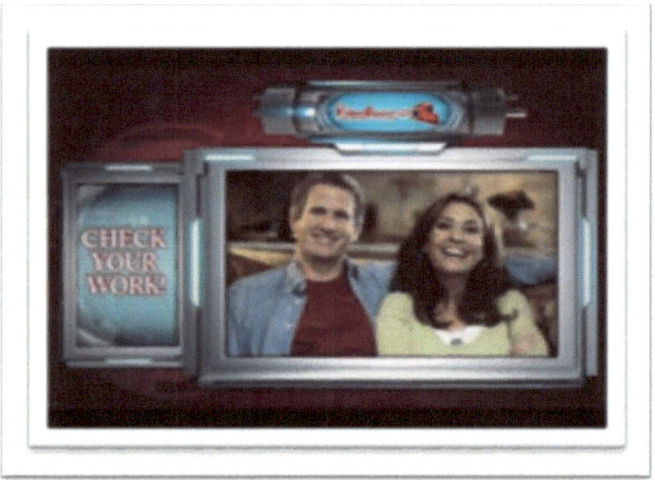

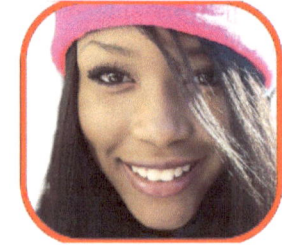

Carl's Assistant: I know you may be excited about your new creation, but it's better to check it before showing it. You may have to go back and re-edit mistakes. It's time for Carl to wrap things up.

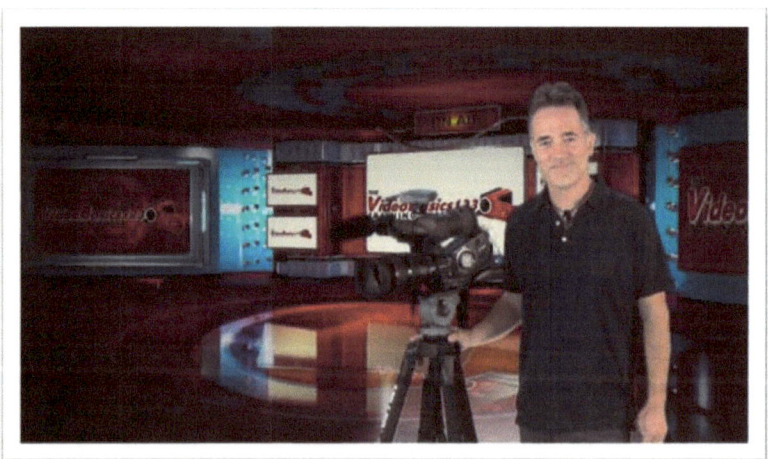

Carl: Alright. So you've watched this DVD and read this workbook now three or four dozen times. It's time to get out there and shoot, edit and communicate. Action!

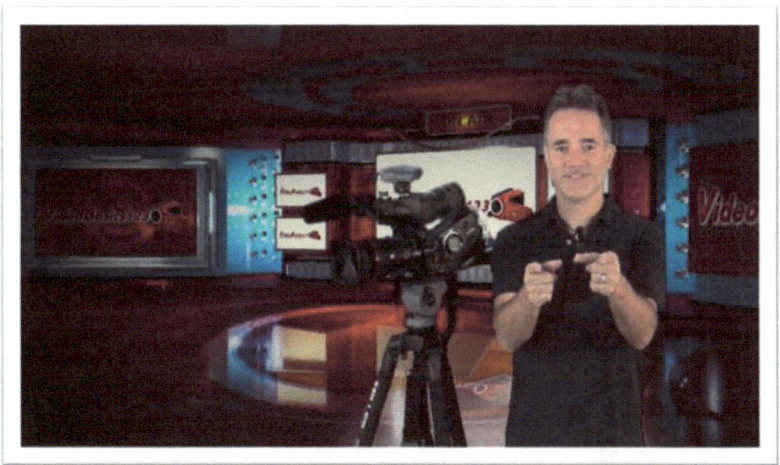

Carl's Assistant: 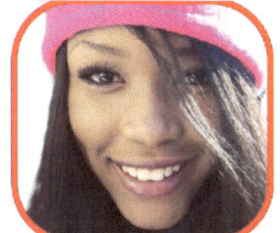 **That's going to do it for the video basics one, two, three training system. As you know you can always go back and review each lesson. If you're still not sure or have questions don't forget to use the video basics one, two, three handy dandy workbook with tips on how to shoot, edit and communicate or go to our website for more information and support. For all of us in the Crown Broadcasting family, see you next time!**

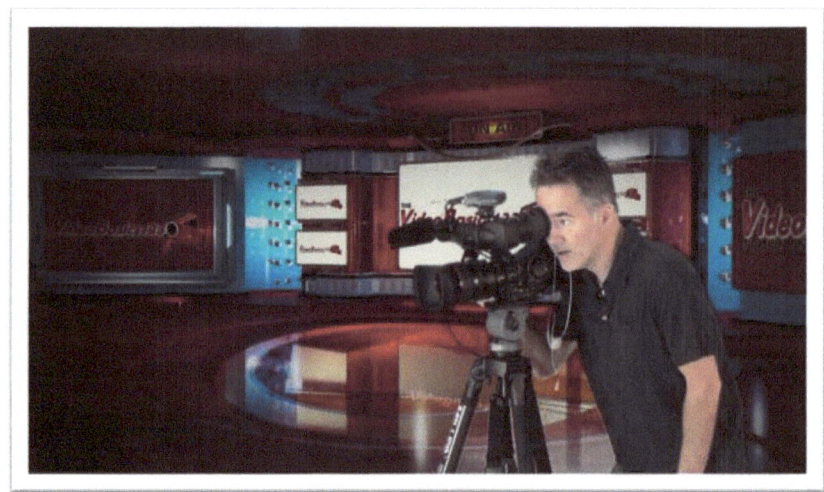

ABOUT CAMERAMAN CARL LEMON

Carl Lemon is a professional well respected videographer specializing in both short and long-form professional video production. He is also a highly decorated television news photographer with more than 20 years of broadcast experience.

Having recorded over an incredible 20,000 hours of footage, Carl has mastered a unique visual style and strong storytelling ability that provides a creative and personalized product to fit any need or objective.

www.ingramcontent.com/pod-product-compliance
Lightning Source LLC
Chambersburg PA
CBHW050745180526
45159CB00003B/1359